6 Skills to expand your English

Stretch

STARTER

Susan Stempleski

Presenting skills consultant:
Ben Shearon

OXFORD
UNIVERSITY PRESS

STRETCH

Stretch teaches listening, speaking, reading, writing, viewing, and presenting skills to prepare you for success in academic and professional life.

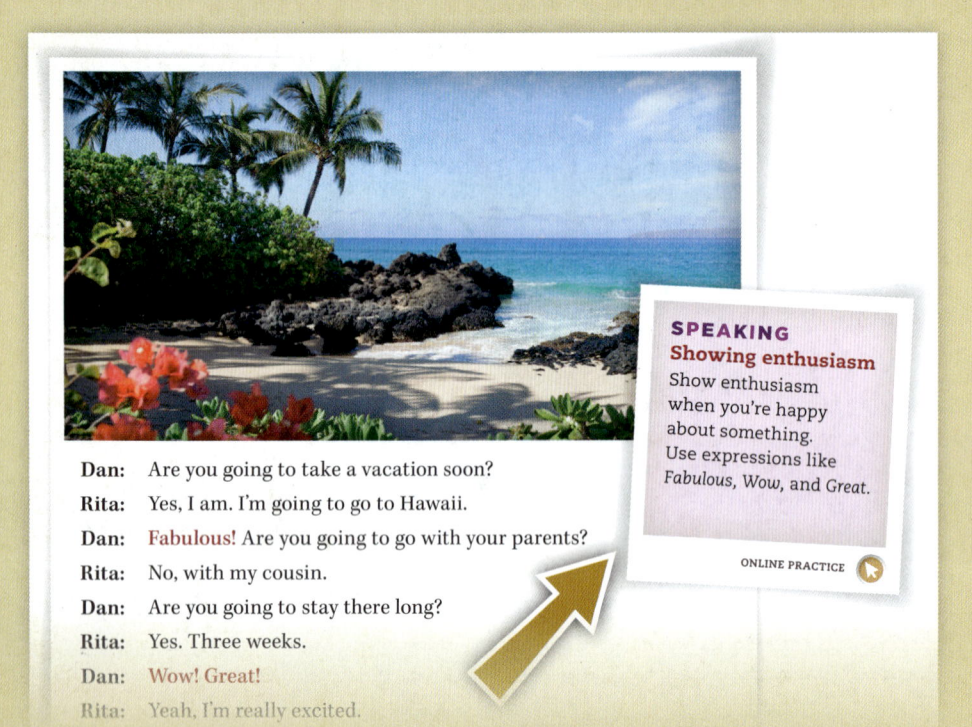

Dan: Are you going to take a vacation soon?
Rita: Yes, I am. I'm going to go to Hawaii.
Dan: Fabulous! Are you going to go with your parents?
Rita: No, with my cousin.
Dan: Are you going to stay there long?
Rita: Yes. Three weeks.
Dan: Wow! Great!
Rita: Yeah, I'm really excited.

SPEAKING
Showing enthusiasm
Show enthusiasm when you're happy about something. Use expressions like *Fabulous*, *Wow*, and *Great*.

ONLINE PRACTICE

Skill Snapshots

are short presentations that highlight the skills taught in *Stretch*. You can find them on most of the Student Book pages. Skill Snapshots ensure you know what you are learning on each page.

Online Practice

deepens your understanding of the information in the Skill Snapshots by providing new presentations for each of the six skills. You will find more than 100 activities you can do any time, anywhere—with automatic grading and feedback on your answers.

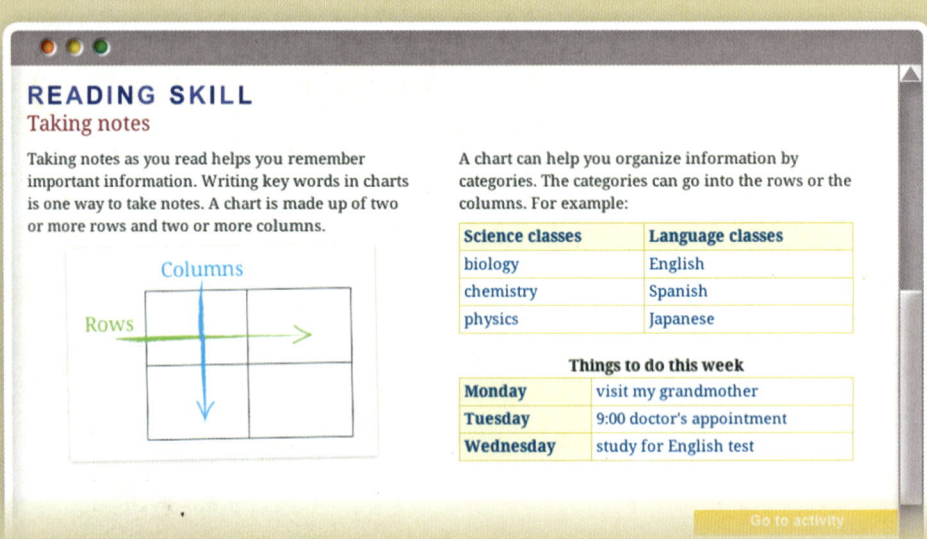

READING SKILL
Taking notes

Taking notes as you read helps you remember important information. Writing key words in charts is one way to take notes. A chart is made up of two or more rows and two or more columns.

A chart can help you organize information by categories. The categories can go into the rows or the columns. For example:

Science classes	Language classes
biology	English
chemistry	Spanish
physics	Japanese

Things to do this week	
Monday	visit my grandmother
Tuesday	9:00 doctor's appointment
Wednesday	study for English test

Go to activity

Use the access code on the inside back cover to log in at
www.oxfordlearn.com

6 Skills to expand your English

5 VIEWING: A weekend in Bali

A Look at the photo and the map, and make predictions. Answer the questions below.

BBC Worldwide Learning

INDONESIA
Bali

1. What is the woman going to do?
2. What is she going to see?
3. Is she going to have fun?

B What does Mohini do in Bali? Check ✓ your answers.
- ☐ plays tennis
- ☐ takes a boat ride
- ☐ goes shopping
- ☐ goes scuba diving
- ☐ sees a lot of fish
- ☐ visits a museum

C Watch again. Complete the sentences. Use words from the box.

VIEWING
Using photos to make predictions
Look at photos and make predictions before you watch. This helps you to understand a video.

ONLINE PRACTICE

Viewing Skills
Research shows that learning English through videos helps you remember more information, develop cross-cultural awareness, and expand your critical thinking. **Viewing Skills**, such as interpreting facial expressions, use BBC Worldwide Learning videos to teach media literacy for 21st-century success.

Presenting Skills help you become a better public speaker. Stretch teaches four types of presenting skills:
1) controlling your body language
2) organizing your ideas
3) designing your message
4) using speech techniques

6 PRESENTING

A Read the presentation. The presenter talks about four places in Portland, Maine. List them.

1. _____
2. _____
3. _____
4. _____

PRESENTING
Making lists and speaking loudly
Make a list to organize your ideas. Add one comment for each point. When you present, speak loudly.

ONLINE PRAC

Come to Portland, Maine, and spend a day like a local. First, go to Becky's Diner for breakfast. Have pancakes with blueberries. Then go

iii

SCOPE AND SEQUENCE

UNIT	VOCABULARY AND LISTENING	SPEAKING	GRAMMAR	READING AND WRITING
1 **Meeting people** Pages 2–7	name, apartment number, email address, etc. **SKILL:** Listening for details (1)	Introductions Pronunciation: Sentence stress **SKILL:** Asking for repetition	To be; subject pronouns; possessive adjectives	Reading: Personal Profile Writing: My personal profile **SKILL:** Brainstorming
2 **Countries and nationalities** Pages 8–13	Country: Australia, Mexico, etc. Nationality: Australian, Mexican, etc. **SKILL:** Listening for details (2)	Where people are from Pronunciation: Contractions **SKILL:** Taking turns in a conversation	Yes/No questions and short answers with be	Reading: New Student Introductions Writing: Favorite foods **SKILL:** Scanning for details
3 **Family** Pages 14–19	husband, sister, mother, etc. **SKILL:** Listening for key words	Talking about family Pronunciation: Question intonation **SKILL:** Asking follow-up questions	Wh- questions with be	Reading: Max Wells Writing: My family **SKILL:** Making an idea map
Self-Assessment Units 1–3 Pages 20–21	Vocabulary and Grammar Reading: Trina's birthday			
4 **Describing people** Pages 22–27	tall, blond hair, green eyes, etc. **SKILL:** Listening for descriptions	Favorite actor Pronunciation: Is he vs. Is she **SKILL:** Showing that you are thinking	Have: affirmative and negative statements; Yes/No questions	Reading: Celebrity Twins Writing: Descriptions of yourself and your family **SKILL:** Using photos to preview a reading
5 **Food and drinks** Pages 28–33	soup, cake, fish, etc. **SKILL:** Listening for a specific purpose	Italian food Pronunciation: Stressing opinions **SKILL:** Expressing likes and dislikes	Simple present: affirmative and negative statements; Yes/No questions	Reading: Chico's Restaurant Writing: Review of a restaurant **SKILL:** Using a T-chart
6 **Things we do** Pages 34–39	studying, shopping, texting, etc. **SKILL:** Making guesses	Describing what you're doing Pronunciation: Linking **SKILL:** Adding information (1)	Present continuous: affirmative and negative statements; Yes/No questions	Reading: A Text Message Writing: Texting **SKILL:** Making guesses
Self-Assessment Units 4–6 Pages 40–41	Vocabulary and Grammar Reading: Dinner plans			

VIEWING BBC Worldwide Learning	PRESENTING	CULTURE TALK!	LEARNING OUTCOMES I can...
Meeting elephants **SKILL:** *Noticing familiar words*	Information about you **SKILL:** *Standing up straight (1)*	A country's popular nicknames	...ask for repetition. ...brainstorm ideas. ...notice familiar words.
Two great cities **SKILL:** *Thinking about the topic*	Introducing a friend **SKILL:** *Looking up (1)*	A country's traditional foods	...listen for details about countries. ...scan for details. ...look up when I give a presentation.
A family business **SKILL:** *Understanding visuals*	This is my family **SKILL:** *Speaking loudly*	Impolite questions	...listen for key words about family. ...ask *Wh-* questions with *be*. ...understand visuals.
Hairstyles **SKILL:** *Using visuals for meaning*	Describing Ed Sheeran **SKILL:** *Using lists*	People with red hair	...show that I'm thinking. ...use photos to preview a reading. ...use lists to organize my ideas.
Hong Kong food tour **SKILL:** *Connecting to the video*	Three good restaurants **SKILL:** *Introducing your topic*	Eating dessert	...express likes and dislikes. ...connect to a video. ...introduce my topic.
Robot doctors **SKILL:** *Taking notes*	Morning routine **SKILL:** *Ending a presentation*	Texting	...add information. ...make guesses when I read. ...take notes as I watch.

SCOPE AND SEQUENCE   v

UNIT	VOCABULARY AND LISTENING	SPEAKING	GRAMMAR	READING AND WRITING
7 **At home** Pages 42–47	living room, kitchen, hall, etc. **SKILL:** Using visuals	Apartment Pronunciation: Word stress **SKILL:** Explaining your reasons	There is/There are; Yes/No questions; prepositions of place	Reading: Strange Houses Writing: A house you know **SKILL:** Writing a topic sentence
8 **Free time activities** Pages 48–53	go to the movies, listen to music, eat out, etc. **SKILL:** Listening for tone (1)	Shopping Pronunciation: Reductions **SKILL:** Showing interest	Simple present: Wh- questions; adverbs of frequency	Reading: How often do you play video games? Writing: Free time activities **SKILL:** Identifying a writer's purpose
9 **Popular sports** Pages 54–59	play volleyball, go snowboarding, do martial arts, etc. **SKILL:** Listening for main ideas	Sports I like **SKILL:** Adding information (2)	Using can for ability Pronunciation: Can vs. can't	Reading: Can you paddleboard? Writing: Sports I can/ can't do **SKILL:** Using and and but
Self-Assessment Units 7–9 Pages 60–61	Vocabulary and Grammar Reading: Carlos's hobbies			
10 **Big events** Pages 62–67	get a job, take guitar lessons, go on a date, etc. **SKILL:** Listening for time phrases	Taking a vacation Pronunciation: going to **SKILL:** Showing enthusiasm	be going to: affirmative and negative statements; Yes/No Questions	Reading: Matson University News Writing: Summer plans **SKILL:** Taking notes
11 **Plans** Pages 68–73	go away, visit a museum, see friends, etc. **SKILL:** Listening for plans	Weekend plans **SKILL:** Accepting an invitation	be going to: Wh- questions Pronunciation: Reduction of are	Reading: Weekend plans in the city Writing: Asking about people's plans **SKILL:** Writing a revision
12 **On vacation** Pages 74–79	rented a car, visited Tarzan Falls, ate delicious food, etc. **SKILL:** Listening for tone (2)	Vacation Pronunciation: Reduction of did you **SKILL:** Responding to news	Simple past	Reading: Mina King Writing: My recent vacation **SKILL:** Using a mind map
Self-Assessment Units 10–12 Pages 80–81	Vocabulary and Grammar Reading: A friendly email			

GRAMMAR REFERENCE
Pages 82–93

GRAMMAR TALK!
Pages 94–105

VIEWING BBC Worldwide Learning	PRESENTING	CULTURE TALK!	LEARNING OUTCOMES I can...
Tiny houses **SKILL:** *Identifying facts and opinions*	Your dream house **SKILL:** *Using visuals*	Unlucky numbers	...use visuals to listen about housing. ...explain my reasons. ...identify facts and opinions.
Chess capital of the world **SKILL:** *Paying attention to numbers*	Free time activities **SKILL:** *Using charts and graphs*	Playing chess	...identify a writer's purpose. ...pay attention to numbers. ...use charts and graphs in a presentation.
Brush boarding **SKILL:** *Asking questions*	An unusual sport **SKILL:** *Supporting ideas with photos*	Some popular sports	...identify sports in conversations. ...use *can* to talk about ability. ...use photos to support my ideas.
Gap year **SKILL:** *Understanding data.*	Taking a gap year **SKILL:** *Standing up straight (2)*	Gap years in different countries	...listen for time phrases about big events. ...show enthusiasm. ...understand data.
A weekend in Bali **SKILL:** *Using photos to make predictions*	A barbecue **SKILL:** *Looking up (2)*	Your weekend plans	...accept an invitation. ...write a revision. ...use photos to make predictions.
Tourist or local? **SKILL:** *Understanding the order of events*	A day in Portland **SKILL:** *Making lists and speaking loudly*	City locals	...respond to news. ...ask and answer *Wh-* questions in the simple past. ...make lists and speak loudly in presentations.

WORD LIST

Pages 106–107

AUDIO AND VIDEO SCRIPTS

Pages 108–113

SCOPE AND SEQUENCE   vii

1 Meeting people

Listening
Listening for details (1)

Speaking
Asking for repetition

Grammar
To be; subject pronouns; possessive adjectives

Writing
Brainstorming

Viewing
Noticing familiar words

Presenting
Standing up straight (1)

1 VOCABULARY AND LISTENING

A Listen and repeat.
CD 1-02

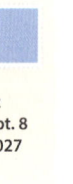

1. name
2. nickname 
3. first name 
4. last name 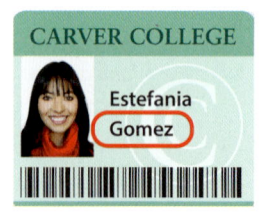
5. address 
6. apartment number 
7. phone number 
8. email address 

B Complete the sentences with the correct words.

1. My _____ is 555-972-0399.
2. My _____ is Alexander Lee.
3. My _____ is Alex.
4. My _____ is alexlee@yakadoo.com.
5. My _____ is 523 Third Avenue, Montreal, QC H3Z 2Y7, Canada.

C Listen and circle the correct information each speaker wants.
CD 1-03

1. a. address
   b. email address
2. a. nickname
   b. name
3. a. address
   b. phone number
4. a. phone number
   b. apartment number
5. a. nickname
   b. last name
6. a. email address
   b. last name

> **LISTENING**
> **Listening for details (1)**
> When you listen for details, you listen for information like names and phone numbers.
>
> ONLINE PRACTICE

D Listen Again. Circle the correct answer.
CD 1-03

1. 22 Baker / Market Street
2. Susanna Chan / Sarah Chang
3. 555-323-6733 / 555-332-6733
4. apartment 2 / apartment 3
5. Susie / Susan
6. SueChan13@gotmail.com / SChan33@coolmail.com

I can... listen for details about personal information. ☐ Very well ☐ Well ☐ Not very well

2

2 SPEAKING

A Complete the conversation with words from the box.

> hello   meet   name   nice   what's

A: Hi.
B: _Hello_.
A: What's your _name_?
B: Daniel. _What's_ your name?
A: Paul. Nice to _meet_ you.
B: It's _nice_ to meet you, too.

B Listen to the conversation. Then practice with a partner.
CD 1-04

SPEAKING
Asking for repetition
Ask for repetition when you don't understand something. Use expressions like *Could you repeat that?* or *Excuse me?*

ONLINE PRACTICE

Mark: Hello, my name's Mark. What's your name?
David: Hi, Mark. I'm David.
Mark: Could you repeat that?
David: Yes, my name is David. Please call me Dave. It's my nickname.
Mark: OK. It's nice to meet you, Dave.
David: Nice to meet you, too.

C Work in pairs. Practice the conversation below with your own information.

A: Hello, my name's _____.
B: Hi, _____. I'm _____.
A: Could you repeat that?
B: Yes, my name's _____.

CULTURE TALK!

In the United States, *Danny* and *Dan* are popular nicknames for *Daniel*. What are some popular nicknames in your country?

D **Pronunciation** **Sentence stress** Listen and repeat.
CD 1-05 We stress important words in sentences.

1. My **name**'s **David**.   2. **Nice** to **meet you**.   3. Could you **repeat** that?

I can... ask for repetition.   ☐ Very well   ☐ Well   ☐ Not very well

UNIT 1   3

3 GRAMMAR

A Listen. Then listen again and repeat.

Grammar Reference page 82

To be; subject pronouns; possessive adjectives

I **am** / **'m** a student.	I **am not** / **'m not** a teacher.
You **are** / **'re** a teacher.	You **are not** / **aren't** a student.
He **is** / **'s** in the classroom.	He **is not** / **isn't** at a restaurant.
She **is** / **'s** Maria.	She **is not** / **isn't** Sarah.
It **is** / **'s** my last name.	It **is not** / **isn't** my first name.
We **are** / **'re** students.	We **are not** / **aren't** teachers.
They **are** / **'re** at school.	They **are not** / **aren't** at home.
What's **your** name?	**My** name's Matthew.
What's **his** name?	**His** name's Ben.
What's **her** name?	**Her** name's Julia.

B Match the questions with the answers.

_b_ 1. What's your name?   a. My nickname's Margie.
_e_ 2. What's your last name?   b. I'm Margaret.
_a_ 3. What's your nickname?   c. Her nickname's Debbie.
_d_ 4. What's his name?   d. His name's Michael.
_c_ 5. What's her nickname?   e. My last name's Hernandez.

C Work in pairs. Ask questions and give answers.

Example: David / Dave
A: What's his name?
B: It's David.
A: What's his nickname?
B: It's Dave.

1. Rick / rickyb@coolmail.com
2. Tina and Sam / Morgan 
3. Steven / 555-495-2268 
4. Kelly Jones / 3134 Green Street, Apartment 9B 
5. James / Jim 
6. your name / your nickname 

D **Grammar Talk!** What's his first name? Student A page 94, Student B page 97.

I can... use the verb *be* and possessive adjectives.   ☐ Very well   ☐ Well   ☐ Not very well

4

4 READING AND WRITING

A Read and listen. Where do you see this kind of information?

Personal Profile

First Name: Jason
Last Name: Jung
Nickname: JJ
email address: mr.jjung@yakadoo.com
phone number: 555-294-0491
Information about you: I'm a student. My school is Kendall College. My favorite class is English. My favorite food is pizza. My birthday is January 10. My favorite movies are *The Life of Pi* and *Star Trek Into Darkness*.

COMMENT

Dan Webber Hi, JJ! How are you?

B Read again. Answer the questions.
1. What's his name?
2. What's his email address?
3. What's his favorite class?
4. What's his favorite food?
5. What are his favorite movies?

WRITING
Brainstorming
Make a list of ideas before you write. This is called brainstorming.

ONLINE PRACTICE

C What information can you put in a personal profile? Brainstorm some ideas.

favorite books   _____   _____

_____   _____   _____

D Complete the personal profile with your information. Add one additional piece of information. Then write a paragraph about you.

First Name: _____
Last Name: _____
Nickname: _____
Email address: _____

Information about you: My name's _____. I am a(n) _____. My favorite food is _____. My favorite _____ is _____. My birthday is _____. My favorite actors are _____ and _____.

I can... brainstorm ideas.   ☐ Very well   ☐ Well   ☐ Not very well

UNIT 1   5

5 VIEWING: Meeting elephants

A Look at the picture and the map. Where is the woman? What do you know about elephants?

B Watch the video. Check ✓ the words you hear.
- ☐ hi
- ☐ welcome
- ☐ thank you
- ☐ name
- ☐ hello
- ☐ favorite
- ☐ baby
- ☐ yes
- ☐ good
- ☐ no
- ☐ address
- ☐ please

> **VIEWING**
> **Noticing familiar words**
> Try to understand familiar words (words you know). This helps you understand words you don't know.
>
> ONLINE PRACTICE

C Watch again. Circle the correct words.
1. The woman's *first / last* name is Mohini.
2. Kuala Gandah (the elephant sanctuary) is *150 / 50* kilometers from Kuala Lumpur.
3. There are 1,200 wild Asian elephants in *the elephant sanctuary / Malaysia*.
4. The baby elephant is six *years / months* old.
5. Elephants are big, but they're *quiet / gentle*.

D What are your favorite animals? Why? Tell a partner.
A: What are your favorite animals?
B: My favorite animals are cats. Cats are pretty, quiet, and smart.

I can... notice familiar words.   ☐ Very well   ☐ Well   ☐ Not very well

6 PRESENTING

A Look at the photos. Who is a good presenter? Who is not a good presenter? Why?

> **PRESENTING**
> **Standing up straight (1)**
> When you give a presentation, stand up straight. You look good and confident.
>
> ONLINE PRACTICE

B Read the presentation to a partner. Stand up straight.

> "My name's Frederico Santos. My nickname's Rico. I'm a student. My birthday is in August. My favorite movies are *Superman* and *The Hobbit*. My favorite TV show is *Sherlock*."

C Complete the chart with information about you.

Name	Nickname	Birthday	Favorite movies	Favorite TV shows

TIP

Before you present to a group, practice with a partner.

D Stand up. Use your notes from Part C. Tell a group about yourself. Remember to stand up straight.

PRESENT

I can... stand up straight when I give a presentation. ☐ Very well ☐ Well ☐ Not very well

2 Countries and nationalities

Listening
Listening for details (2)

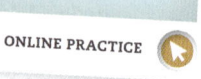

Speaking
Taking turns in a conversation

Grammar
Yes/No questions with *be*

Reading
Scanning for details

Viewing
Thinking about the topic

Presenting
Looking up (1)

1 VOCABULARY AND LISTENING

A Listen and repeat.
CD 1-08

1. Country: Australia
   Nationality: Australian
2. Country: Brazil 
   Nationality: Brazilian
3. Country: Vietnam 
   Nationality: Vietnamese
4. Country: Japan 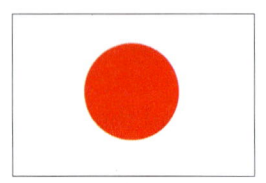
   Nationality: Japanese
5. Country: South Korea 
   Nationality: South Korean
6. Country: the United Kingdom 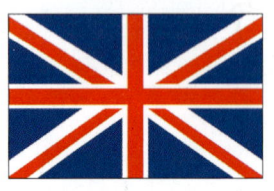
   Nationality: British
7. Country: the United States 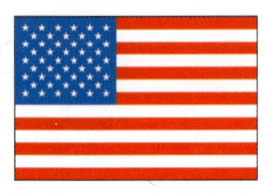
   Nationality: American
8. Country: Mexico 
   Nationality: Mexican

B Complete the sentences with the correct words.
ONLINE PRACTICE

1. I'm from Australia. I'm _____.
2. Marta is from Mexico. She's _____.
3. Simon is from _____. He's British.
4. Jim and Dan are from _____. They're American.
5. Joao and Luis are from Brazil. They're _____.

C Listen and check ✓ what each speaker talks about.
CD 1-09

1. ☑ a. country
   ☐ b. nationality
2. ☑ a. country
   ☐ b. nationality
3. ☐ a. country
   ☑ b. nationality
4. ☑ a. country
   ☐ b. nationality

> **LISTENING**
> **Listening for details (2)**
> When you listen for details, you listen for information like countries and nationalities.
>
> ONLINE PRACTICE

D Listen Again Number the pictures from *1–4*.
CD 1-09

a.  (Mexico)   b. 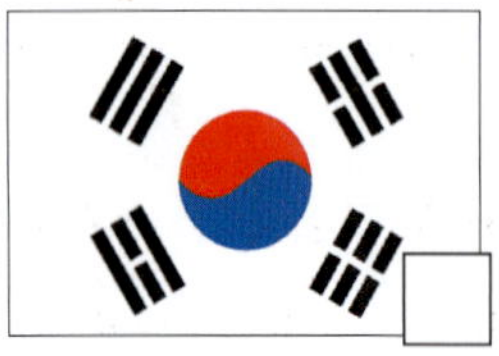 (South Korea)   c.  (Vietnam)   d.  (Brazil)

> **I can...** listen for details about countries.   ☐ Very well   ☐ Well   ☐ Not very well

8

2 SPEAKING

A Match the questions and answers.

___ 1. Are you the teacher? a. I'm Tina.
___ 2. What's your name? b. I'm from Japan.
___ 3. Where are you from? c. No, I'm from South Korea.
___ 4. Are you Vietnamese? d. No, I'm a student.

B Listen to the conversation. Then practice with a partner.
CD 1-10

Steve: Hi, are you in this class?
Gina: Yes, I am.
Steve: What's your name?
Gina: My name's Gina.
Steve: Nice to meet you. I'm Steve. Where are you from, Gina?
Gina: I'm from Brazil. How about you? Are you British?
Steve: No, I'm not. I'm Australian.

> **SPEAKING**
> **Taking turns in a conversation**
> To take turns in a conversation, ask questions like *Where are you from?*, *And you?*, or *How about you?*
>
> ONLINE PRACTICE

C Work in pairs. Practice the conversation below with your own information.

A: Hi, my name's _____. What's your name?
B: I'm _____. Where are you from, _____?
A: I'm from _____. How about you? Are you _____?
B: No, I'm not. I'm _____.

D Pronunciation Contractions Listen and repeat. Notice how the contractions are pronounced.
CD 1-11

What's your name?   My **name's** Elisa. Where are you from, Pedro?
I'm Pedro. **What's** your name?   **I'm** from Mexico. How about you?

> **I can...** ask questions to take turns in a conversation. ☐ Very well ☐ Well ☐ Not very well

UNIT 2   9

3 GRAMMAR

A Listen. Then listen again and repeat.

Grammar Reference page 83

Yes/No questions and short answers with *be*		
Are you South Korean?	Yes, **I am**.	No, **I'm not**.
Is he Chinese?	Yes, **he is**.	No, **he isn't**.
Are you Brazilian?	Yes, **we are**.	No, **we aren't**.
Are they American?	Yes, **they are**.	No, **they aren't**.

B Match the questions with the answers.

___ 1. Is Peter American?
___ 2. Are Miguel and Sonia from Mexico?
___ 3. Are you from Japan?
___ 4. Is she British?
___ 5. Are you and Lin from China?

a. No, she isn't. She's American.
b. Yes, he is.
c. Yes, we are.
d. No, they aren't. They're from Brazil.
e. No, I'm not. I'm from Vietnam.

C Work in pairs. Ask questions and give answers.

Example:
Sam Tran
A: Is he South Korean?
B: No, he isn't.
A: Is he Vietnamese?
B: Yes, he is.

Rosa Lopez

Sam and Tara Nelson

Hana Park

Nicki Watts and Meg Reilly

Hiro Ito

Eduardo Diaz

D **Grammar Talk!** Where's he from? Student A page 94, Student B page 97.

I can... ask and answer *Yes/No* questions with *be*. ☐ Very well ☐ Well ☐ Not very well

4 READING AND WRITING

A Read and listen. What is the event?

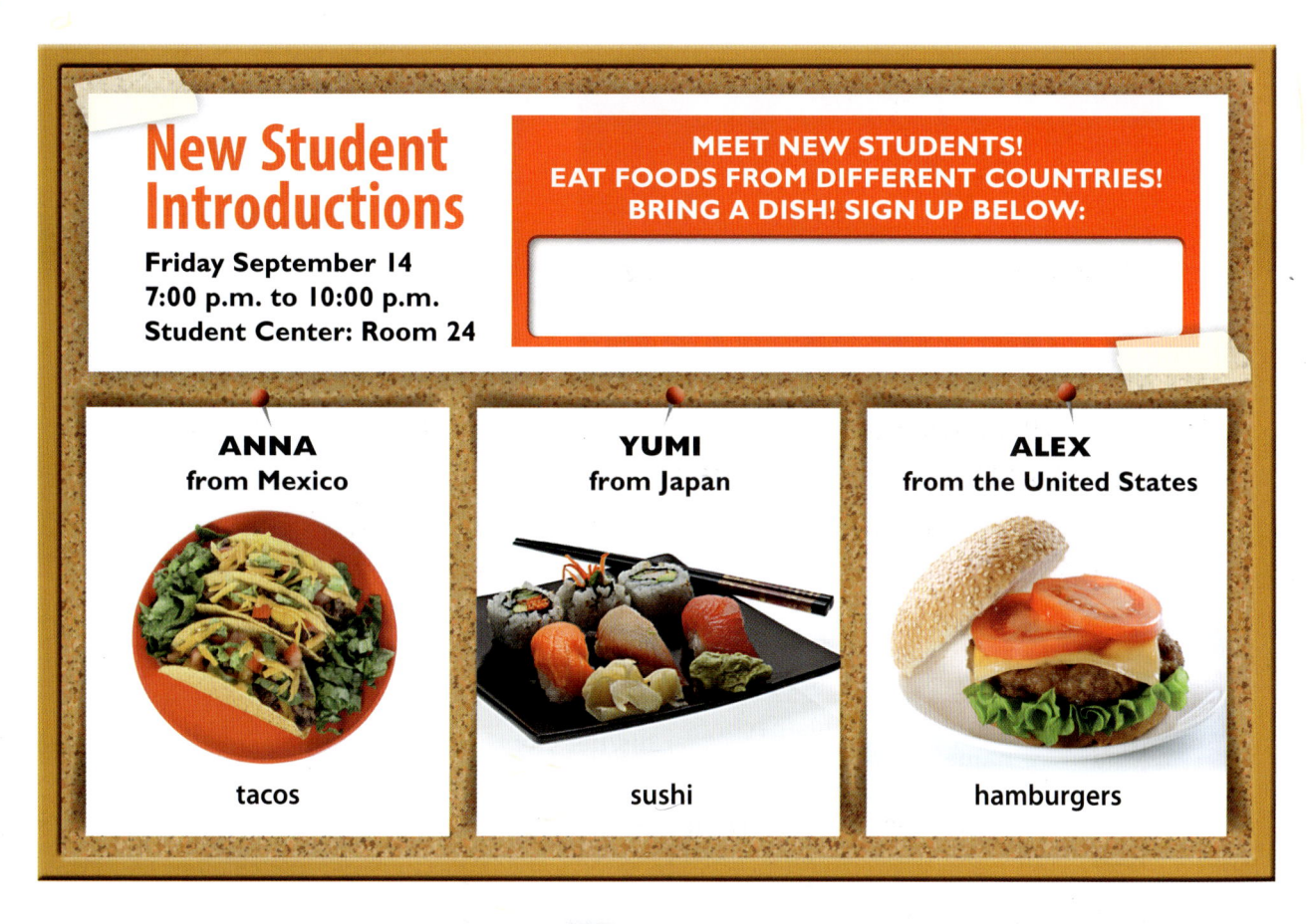

New Student Introductions
Friday September 14
7:00 p.m. to 10:00 p.m.
Student Center: Room 24

**MEET NEW STUDENTS!
EAT FOODS FROM DIFFERENT COUNTRIES!
BRING A DISH! SIGN UP BELOW:**

ANNA from Mexico — tacos

YUMI from Japan — sushi

ALEX from the United States — hamburgers

B Read again. Answer the questions.
1. What day is the event?
2. What time is it?
3. Where is it?
4. What countries is the food from?
5. Where is sushi from?

C What are four of your favorite foods? List foods from other countries. Where are they from?

Food	From
kimchi	South Korea
_____	_____
_____	_____
_____	_____

**READING
Scanning for details**
When you scan a text, you look at it quickly to find details like days and times.

ONLINE PRACTICE

CULTURE TALK!
Feijoada is a traditional Brazilian dish made with beans. What is a traditional dish in your country?

D Write sentences about three foods that you like.

Three of my favorite foods are _____, _____, and _____. _____ is from _____. _____ is from _____. _____ is from _____.

I can... scan for details. ☐ Very well ☐ Well ☐ Not very well

UNIT 2   11

5 VIEWING: Two great cities

A Look at the pictures. What do you know about these cities?

Seoul — *South Korea*

São Paulo — *Brazil*

B Watch the video. Check ✓ what each person talks about.

Person	his/her name	his/her nationality	his/her city	his/her job
#1	✓ Ana Paula	Brazilian	Sao Paulo	
#2		South Korean		
#3				waiter

> **VIEWING**
> **Thinking about the topic**
> Before you watch, ask, What do I know about the topic? This helps you to understand a video.
>
> ONLINE PRACTICE

C Watch again. Read the questions. Circle *Yes* or *No*.

1. Is Ana Paula a student? — Yes — No
2. Is Cho Sung-hoon an auctioneer? — **Yes** — No
3. Is the fish market big? — **Yes** — No
4. Is Yoon Soo-yeon from Hong Kong? — Yes — **No**
5. Is Yoon Soo-yeon a waiter? — **Yes** — No

D Talk to three classmates. Complete the chart with information about them.

	name	nationality	city	favorite food
1.	Romina	Iranian	R...	kiwis
2.				
3.				

I can... think about the topic before I watch. ☐ Very well ☐ Well ☐ Not very well

6 PRESENTING

A Look at the pictures. Who is a good presenter? Who is a bad presenter? Why?

PRESENTING
Looking up (1)
Look up when you are making a presentation. This helps you connect with your audience.

ONLINE PRACTICE

B Read the presentation to a partner. Remember to look up.

"Nice to meet you all. I'm Michael and I'm American. This is my classmate, Julia. She's from the United States, too. I'm from New York, and she's from Los Angeles. We both love soccer very much."

C Ask and answer questions with a partner. Take notes below.

Name _____
From _____
Lives in _____
Favorite food _____
Other information _____

TIP
Look down quickly to read your notes, and then look up at the audience again.

D Stand up. Tell a group about you and your partner. Remember to look up.

I can... look up when I give a presentation. ☐ Very well ☐ Well ☐ Not very well

3 Family

Listening
Listening for key words

Speaking
Asking follow-up questions

Grammar
Wh- questions with be

Writing
Making an idea map

Viewing
Understanding visuals

Presenting
Speaking loudly

1 VOCABULARY AND LISTENING

A Listen and repeat.
CD 1-14

1. husband
2. wife
3. father
4. mother
5. son
6. daughter
7. brother
8. sister

Bill   Nina   Peter   Cindy

B Complete what the people say with the correct words.

1. Bill: Nina is my _wife_.
2. Nina: Bill is my _life_.
3. Nina: Cindy is my _____.
4. Cindy: Peter is my _7_.
5. Peter: Nina is my _4_.

C Listen and check ✓ the words that you hear.
CD 1-15

1. ☐ father   ✓ friend   ✓ brother   ☐ sister
2. ☐ brothers ☐ teachers ✓ sisters   ✓ friends
3. ☐ father   ☐ sister   ✓ mother   ✓ teacher
4. ✓ wife   ☐ brother   ✓ sister   ☐ mother
5. ☐ father   ✓ husband   ☐ son   ✓ brother

> **LISTENING**
> **Listening for key words**
> Key words are important words. Pay attention to words that show relationships, like *mother, wife, friend*.
>
> ONLINE PRACTICE

D *Listen Again* Check *Yes* or *No*.
CD 1-15

	Yes	No
1. Is Marcus her friend?	☐	✓
2. Are Sara and Michelle his sisters?	✓	☐
3. Is Kim her mother?	✓	☐
4. Is Medina his sister?	☐	✓
5. Is Carlos her brother?	☐	✓

I can... listen for key words about family.   ☐ Very well   ☐ Well   ☐ Not very well

14

2 SPEAKING

A Complete the conversation with the sentences from the box.

| He's from Mexico. | He's 42. | His name is Alex. | That's my father. |

1. A: Who's that?   B: *That's my father.*
2. A: What's his name?   B: *His name is Alex*
3. A: Where's he from?   B: *He's from Mexico*
4. A: How old is he?   B: *He's 42.*

B Listen to the conversation. Then practice with a partner.
CD 1-16

Alice: Nice photos. Hey, who's that?
Mia: That's my brother.
Alice: What's his name?
Mia: His name's Eric.
Alice: How old is he?
Mia: He's 26.
Alice: Is he married?
Mia: No, he isn't. He's single.

**SPEAKING
Asking follow-up questions**
Ask follow-up questions like the ones in red to continue a conversation and find out more information.

ONLINE PRACTICE

C **Pronunciation** Question intonation Listen and repeat.
CD 1-17
Yes/No questions go up at the end. *Wh-* questions go down at the end.

1. Is he your brother? ↗
2. What's his name? ↘

D Work in pairs. Practice the conversation below with your own information. Show your partner a photo if you have one.

A: Who's that?
B: That's my _____.
A: What's _____ name?
B: _____ name's _____.
A: How old is _____?

CULTURE TALK!

In the United States, it's not polite to ask *How old are you?* unless you know the person well. How about in your country?

I can... ask follow-up questions. ☐ Very well ☐ Well ☐ Not very well

UNIT 3   15

3 GRAMMAR

A Listen. Then listen again and repeat.

Grammar Reference page 84

Wh- questions with be	
What's your name?	My name's Ken.
Where are you from?	I'm from New York.
How are you?	I'm fine.
Who's that?	That's my sister.
How old is she?	She's 16.
Who are they?	They're my parents.

B Match the questions with the answers.

___ 1. How are you?   a. He's 28.
___ 2. Who's that?   b. He's from Mexico.
___ 3. What's his name?   c. I'm fine.
___ 4. How old is he?   d. His name's Pedro.
___ 5. Where's he from?   e. That's my husband.

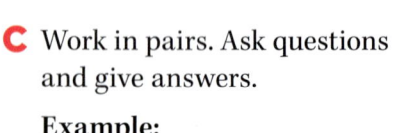

C Work in pairs. Ask questions and give answers.

Example:

brother / Luiz / single

A: Who's that?   A: What's his name?   A: Is he married?
B: That's my brother.   B: His name's Luiz.   B: No, he isn't. He's single.

1. mother / Yukiko / Tokyo 
2. wife / Cara / Mexico 
3. sister / single / 22

4. husband / Steven / the U.K.
5. brother / Dan / single 
6. Linda / married / 26 

D **Grammar Talk!** Who's that? Student A page 95, Student B page 98.

I can... ask Wh- questions with be. ☐ Very well ☐ Well ☐ Not very well

16

4 READING AND WRITING

A Read and listen. Where do you see this kind of information?

Max Wells

Profile
Photos (51)
Notes
Friends

This is my family 20 years ago. In this picture, my mother, Linda, is 32, and my father, Ed, is 34. I'm six years old. My brother is two. His name's Ben. My sister is nine. Her name's Petra. We're very happy. Ben is 22 now. He isn't married. Petra is 29 years old and is married. She has a son and a daughter. I'm 26 now, and I'm single.

B Read again. Answer the questions.

1. Who are Linda and Ed?   They're his _____.
2. How old is Max in the photo? He's _____.
3. Who is Ben?   He's his _____.
4. Who is Petra?   She's his _____.
5. How old is Petra now?   She's _____.

C Make an idea map like the one below for three family members. Write information about each person.

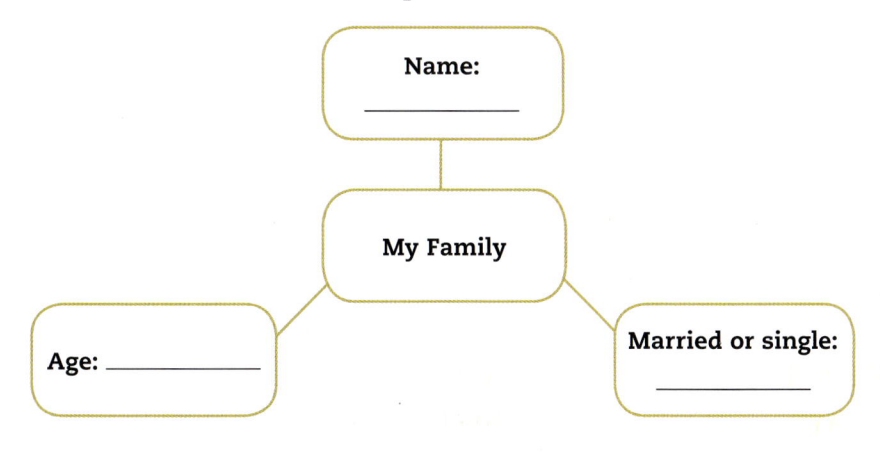

Name: _____

My Family

Age: _____

Married or single: _____

WRITING
Making an idea map
Making an idea map helps develop note-taking, planning, and creativity. Make an idea map to organize your writing.

ONLINE PRACTICE

D Write sentences about your family.

_____ is my _____. He/She is _____ years old.
_____
_____.

> **I can...** use an idea map to organize my writing. ☐ Very well ☐ Well ☐ Not very well

UNIT 3   17

5 VIEWING: A family business

A Look at the pictures. What do people do at amusement parks? At water parks?

amusement park

water park

B Watch the video without sound. Answer the questions.

1. Where does Pace live?
   a. in an amusement park
   b. in a big house
2. Who does Pace live with?
   a. his parents, brothers, and sisters
   b. his parents and grandparents
3. Is Pace happy?
   a. Yes.
   b. No.

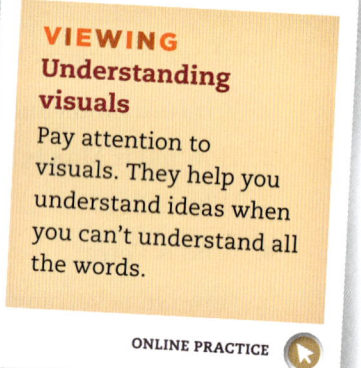

> **VIEWING**
> **Understanding visuals**
> Pay attention to visuals. They help you understand ideas when you can't understand all the words.
>
> ONLINE PRACTICE

C Watch again. Check your answers in Part B.

D Watch again. Complete the sentences about Pace's family. Use words from the box.

| brothers | grandparents ✓ | sisters | grandmother | mother | grandfather | father |

1. His _grandparents_ own the park.
2. Ken is his _grandfather_.
3. Violet is his _grandm_.
4. His mother has five _brothers_ and _sisters_.
5. His _mother_ is a salesperson.
6. His _father_ is a manager.

E Discuss the questions with a partner.

1. What are some amusement parks or water parks near where you live?
2. Do you ever go to amusement parks or water parks? What are your favorites? Why?

I can... understand visuals. ☐ Very well ☐ Well ☐ Not very well

6 PRESENTING

A Listen to two speakers give the same presentation. (You will just hear the beginning of the presentation.) Which one is a good presenter? Why? Check ✓ your answer.

☐ Speaker 1   ☐ Speaker 2

B Read the presentation to a partner. Speak more loudly than you normally do.

> **PRESENTING**
> **Speaking loudly**
> When you give a presentation, speak loudly (120%–150% of your normal volume). The audience needs to hear you clearly.
>
> ONLINE PRACTICE

"My name's Hannah. This is a photo of my family. Here is my daughter, Lily. She's ten years old. And that's my son, Ted. He's five. Behind my daughter is my father. His name is Frank. And that's my mother, Audrey. That's my husband behind my mother. His name is Matt.

And here's a photo of my sisters. This is Emma, in the blue shirt. She's 24. She and her husband have a one-year-old son. And this is my other sister, Annie. She's 17. She's the baby of the family."

C Write a presentation about your family. You can use your ideas from page 17.

_____
_____
_____
_____

TIP
Show your audience some pictures of your family.

D Stand up. Tell a group about your family. Remember to speak loudly.

I can... speak loudly when I give a presentation.   ☐ Very well   ☐ Well   ☐ Not very well

Self-Assessment

1 VOCABULARY

Circle the correct word or words to complete each sentence.

1. My *email address* / *address* / *name* is Marta.
2. I'm Kim Park. My *last name* / *first name* / *name* is Park.
3. My *phone number* / *email address* / *apartment number* is 555-251-0324.
4. My *address* / *phone number* / *apartment number* is 9.

I can... understand vocabulary about personal information. (Unit 1)

5. Toshi is from Japan. He's *Japan* / *Japanese*.
6. Brian is from the U.K. He's *British* / *Britain*.
7. Luis and Carlo are from Brazil. They're *Brazil* / *Brazilian*.

I can... understand vocabulary about countries and nationalities. (Unit 2)

8. This is my *brother* / *sister* / *daughter*. His name's Marcus.
9. My *husband* / *wife* / *son* is from South Korea. Her name's Mina.
10. We have two *sons* / *husbands* / *mothers*. Their names are Michael and James.

I can... understand vocabulary about family. (Unit 3)

2 GRAMMAR

1. I *am* / *is* / *are* a student.
2. This is Anna. *He* / *She* / *It* is my roommate.
3. This is my friend. *He* / *His* / *She* name is Mark.

I can... use the verb *be* and possessive adjectives. (Unit 1)

4. *You are* / *Are you* / *You* American?
5. *Am John* / *Is John* / *Are John* Chinese?
6. *Is Tina* / *Are Tina* / *Tina is* from Brazil?

I can... ask and answer *Yes/No* questions with *be*. (Unit 2)

7. *Who is* / *Who* / *Who are* that?
8. How old *she is* / *she* / *is she*?
9. *What* / *What's* / *What are* your name?
10. *Where is* / *Where are* / *Where* Ken from?

I can... ask *Wh-* questions with *be*. (Unit 3)

Units 1-3

3 READING

A Read and listen to the information. What is the writer's name?

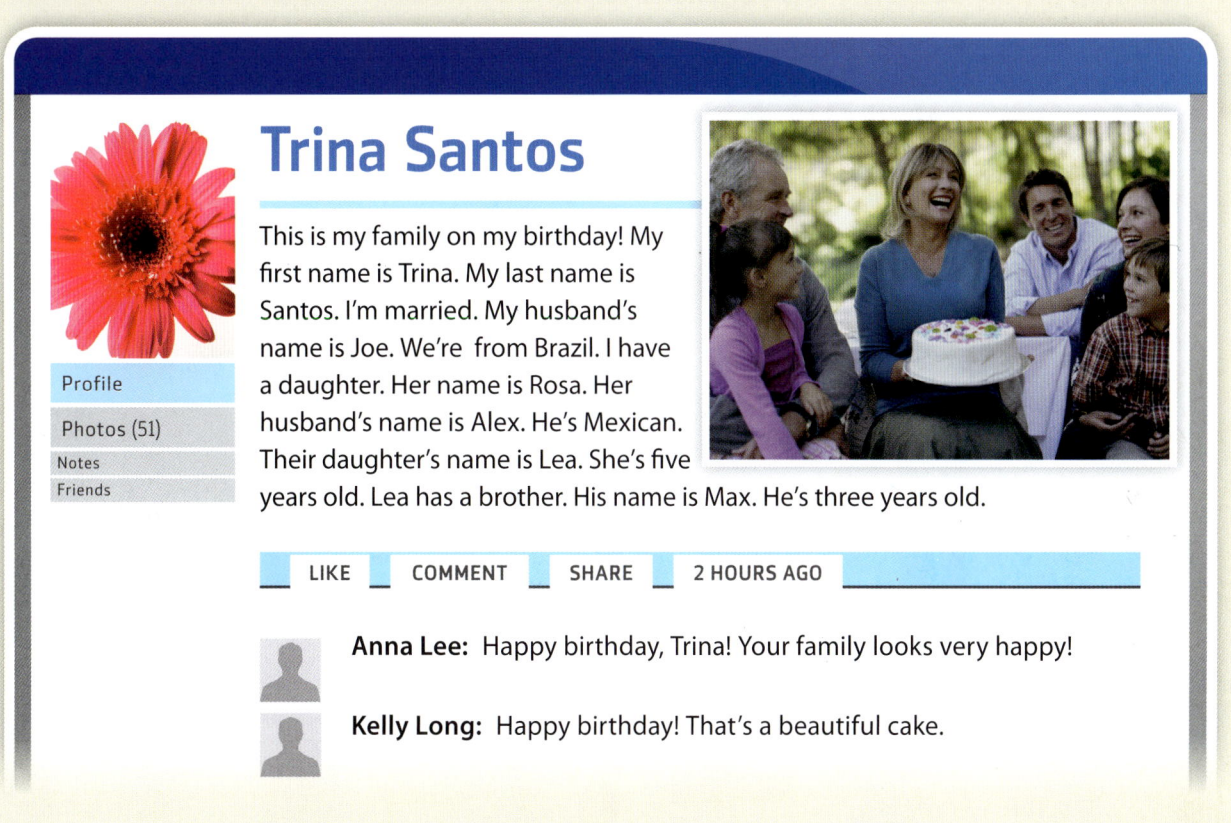

Trina Santos

Profile
Photos (51)
Notes
Friends

This is my family on my birthday! My first name is Trina. My last name is Santos. I'm married. My husband's name is Joe. We're from Brazil. I have a daughter. Her name is Rosa. Her husband's name is Alex. He's Mexican. Their daughter's name is Lea. She's five years old. Lea has a brother. His name is Max. He's three years old.

LIKE   COMMENT   SHARE   2 HOURS AGO

Anna Lee: Happy birthday, Trina! Your family looks very happy!

Kelly Long: Happy birthday! That's a beautiful cake.

B Read each statement. Write **T** (true) or **F** (false). Correct the false statements.

___ 1. Trina's last name is Silva.
___ 2. Joe is Trina's husband.
___ 3. Alex is from Brazil.
___ 4. Lea is Trina's daughter.
___ 5. Max is three years old.

C Answer the questions.

1. Who is Rosa?   She's Trina's _____.
2. Who is Joe?   He's Trina's _____.
3. Who is Alex?   He's Rosa's _____.
4. Where is Alex from?   He's from _____.
5. How old is Lea?   She's _____ years old.

D Tell a partner about your family.

My sister's name is Laura. She's 17 years old.

SELF-ASSESSMENT | UNITS 1–3   21

4 Describing people

Listening
Listening for descriptions

Speaking
Showing you are thinking

Grammar
Have: Yes/No questions

Reading
Using photos to preview a reading

Viewing
Using visuals for meaning

Presenting
Using lists

1 VOCABULARY AND LISTENING

A Listen and repeat.
CD 1-22

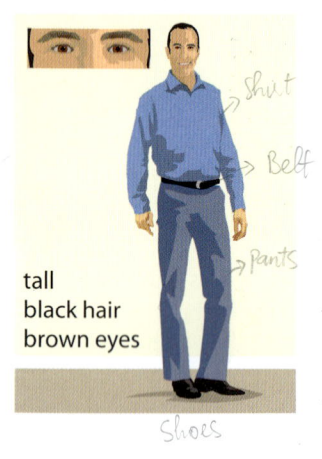

tall
black hair
brown eyes

short
blond hair
blue eyes

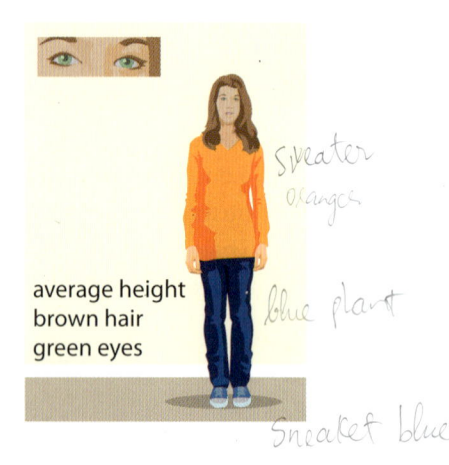

average height
brown hair
green eyes

B Circle the correct words.
ONLINE PRACTICE

1. a. short
   b. tall
   c. average height

2. a. brown hair
   b. blond hair
   c. black hair

3. a. brown eyes
   b. green eyes
   c. blue eyes

> **LISTENING**
> **Listening for descriptions**
> When you listen to descriptions of people, listen for adjectives, such as *tall*, *short*, *brown*, and *blue*.
>
> ONLINE PRACTICE

C Listen to the descriptions. Check ✓ the information you hear for each person.
CD 1-23

1. ✓ hair ☐ height
2. ☐ hair ✓ eyes
3. ☐ eyes ✓ height
4. ✓ eyes ☐ hair

D Listen Again. Check *True*, *False*, or *I don't know*.
CD 1-23

		True	False	I don't know
1.	**Kelly** black hair	✓	☐	☐
2.	**Michael** brown hair	☐	☐	✓
3.	**Ella** tall	☐	✓	☐
4.	**Robert** blond hair	☐	☐	✓

▶ **I can...** listen for descriptions of people. ☐ Very well ☐ Well ☐ Not very well

22

2 SPEAKING

A Match the questions and answers.

___ 1. Does she have dark hair? a. No, she's short.
___ 2. Is she tall? b. Yes, he does.
___ 3. Does he have curly hair? c. No, he's tall.
___ 4. Is he short? d. No, she has blond hair.

B Listen to the conversation. Then practice with a partner.

Jane: Who's your favorite actor?
Katrina: Guess.
Jane: OK. Is he tall?
Katrina: No, he isn't tall. He's average height.
Jane: Does he have blond hair?
Katrina: No, he doesn't. He has brown hair.
Jane: How old is he?
Katrina: Um, I think he's about 35.
Jane: Is it James Franco?
Katrina: Yes, it is!

SPEAKING
Showing you are thinking
To show that you are thinking, use words like *well* and *um*. It makes you sound more natural.

ONLINE PRACTICE

C **Pronunciation** *Is he* vs. *Is she* Listen and repeat. Notice the pronunciation of *is he* and *is she*.

1. **Is he** tall?
2. **Is she** tall?
3. How old **is he**?
4. How old **is she**?

D Work in pairs. Practice the conversation below with your own information. Ask about your partner's favorite actor.

A: Is your favorite actor _____? B: _____?
A: Does he/she have _____ hair? B: Yes he/she does. / No, he/she doesn't.
A: How old is he/she? B: Um, I think he's/she's about _____.
A: Is it _____? B: Yes, it is! / No, it isn't.

▶ **I can...** show that I'm thinking. ☐ Very well ☐ Well ☐ Not very well

UNIT 4 23

3 GRAMMAR

A Listen. Then listen again and repeat.

Grammar Reference page 85

Have: affirmative and negative statements; Yes/No questions

I **have** brown hair.	**Do** you **have** blond hair?
I **don't have** black hair.	Yes, I **do**. / No, I **don't**.
She **has** blue eyes.	**Does** she **have** green eyes?
She **doesn't have** brown eyes.	Yes, she **does**. / No, she **doesn't**.

NOTE:
- Use contractions in speaking; don't = do not; doesn't = does not

B Match the questions with the answers.

___ 1. Does he have brown hair?   a. Yes, I do.
___ 2. Does she have blond hair?   b. Yes, she does.
___ 3. Do they have black hair?   c. No, he doesn't. He has blue eyes.
___ 4. Do you have blue eyes?   d. No, he doesn't.
___ 5. Does he have brown eyes?   e. Yes, they do.

C Work in pairs. Ask questions and give answers.

Example:

blond hair / green eyes

A: Does he have blond hair?
B: No, he doesn't. He has brown hair.
A: Does he have green eyes?
B: Yes, he does.

Example:

blond hair / green eyes

A: Does she have blond hair?
B: Yes, she does.
A: Does she have green eyes?
B: No, she doesn't.

1. brown hair / brown eyes
2. black hair / brown eyes 
3. brown hair / blue eyes 
4. blond hair / brown eyes 
5. black hair / blue eyes 
6. brown hair / green eyes 

D Grammar Talk! That's Sarah. Student A page 95, Student B page 98.

I can... ask and answer Yes/No questions with *have*.   ☐ Very well   ☐ Well   ☐ Not very well

24

4 READING AND WRITING

A Look at the photos. What do you think this article is about? Read and listen.

Celebrity Twins

You might know the actor Scarlett Johansson. Do you know she has a twin brother? Scarlett and her twin, Hunter, look very different. Scarlett is short. She is 5 feet 3 inches (1.60 meters) tall. Her brother is tall. He is 6 feet 3 inches (1.90 meters) tall. Scarlett has blond hair, and her brother has brown hair. Scarlett has green eyes, and her brother has brown eyes.

Actors Aaron and Shawn Ashmore are identical twins. They look exactly alike. They both have brown hair and blue eyes. They are both tall, too. Shawn is 5 feet 11 inches (1.80 meters) tall. His brother Aaron is 6 feet (1.82 meters) tall. Shawn is famous for the *X-Men* movies. He plays the character Iceman. Aaron is an actor, too. He is famous for the TV shows *Smallville* and *Warehouse 13*.

B Read again. Answer the questions.
1. Does Hunter have blond hair?
2. Is Hunter short?
3. Does Hunter have blue eyes?
4. What is the color of Aaron and Shawn's eyes?
5. Are Aaron and Shawn short?

C Write descriptions of yourself and one family member. Choose a family member who looks like you or a family member who looks different from you.

Name	Height	Hair	Eyes
_____	_____	_____	_____
_____	_____	_____	_____

READING
Using photos to preview a reading
When you read, look at the photos to preview the reading. What do the photos tell you about the reading?

ONLINE PRACTICE

D Do you and your family member look alike or different? Choose a set of sentences below. Complete the sentences with information from Part C.

Choice 1: My _____ and I look **alike**. We are _____. We have _____ hair and _____ eyes.

Choice 2: My _____ and I look **different**. I am _____, and my _____ is _____. I have _____, and my _____ has _____.

I can... use photos to preview a reading. ☐ Very well ☐ Well ☐ Not very well

5 VIEWING: Hairstyles

A Look at the pictures. Talk about each person's hair. Do you like it?

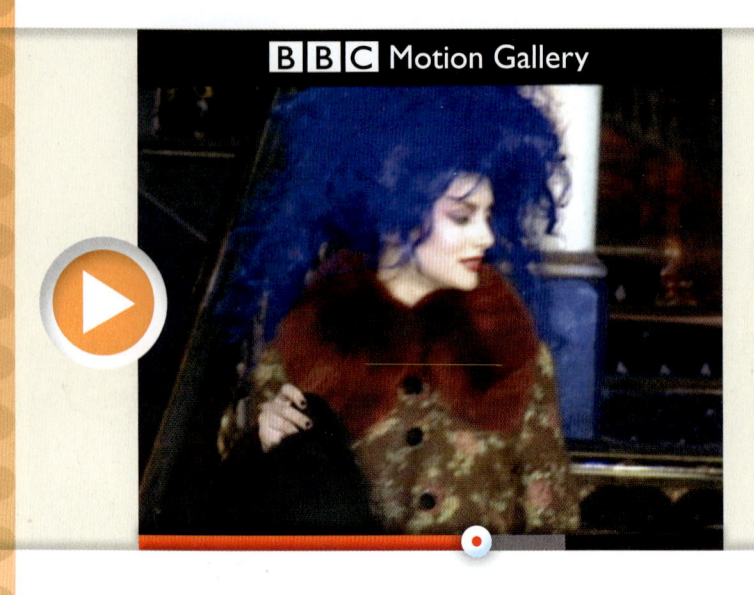

B Match each word with the correct picture. Then watch the video to check your answers.

_d_ 1. mustache   _f_ 3. bun   _e_ 5. straight hair
_b_ 2. wig   _c_ 4. beard   _a_ 6. braids

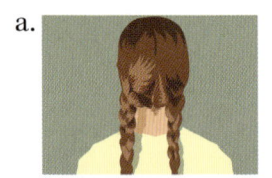

VIEWING
Using visuals for meaning
Look carefully at visuals (pictures). They can help you understand new words.

ONLINE PRACTICE

C Watch again. Complete the sentences. Use words from the box.

| Asian | brown | fun | African | red | short |

1. You can have long or _____ hair.
2. The Hama people of Ethiopia dye their hair _____.
3. The Masai people of Kenya dye their hair _____ on special days.
4. _____ people have oval hair strands.
5. _____ people have round hair strands.
6. Wigs are _____ and fashionable.

CULTURE TALK!
Only 1% of people in the world have red hair. How many people with red hair do you know?

D Write the numbers. Then compare your answers with a partner.
How many students in your class have . . . ?

___ long hair   ___ no hair   ___ braids   ___ short hair   ___ a beard   ___ curly hair

I can... use visuals to learn new vocabulary.   ☐ Very well   ☐ Well   ☐ Not very well

26

6 PRESENTING

A Read the information about Ed Sheeran. Write the correct words in the chart below.

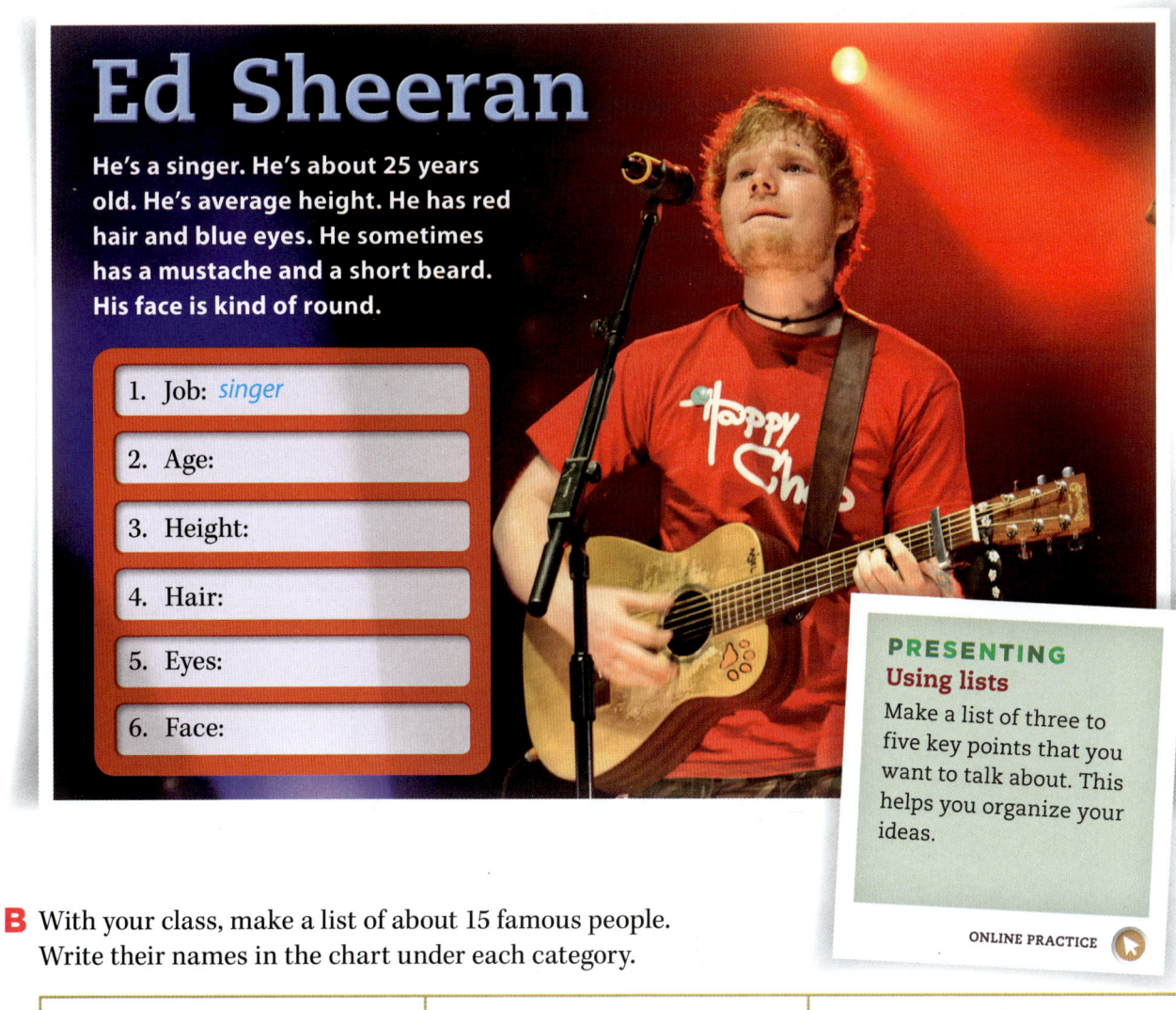

Ed Sheeran

He's a singer. He's about 25 years old. He's average height. He has red hair and blue eyes. He sometimes has a mustache and a short beard. His face is kind of round.

1. Job: *singer*
2. Age:
3. Height:
4. Hair:
5. Eyes:
6. Face:

PRESENTING
Using lists
Make a list of three to five key points that you want to talk about. This helps you organize your ideas.

ONLINE PRACTICE

B With your class, make a list of about 15 famous people. Write their names in the chart under each category.

Music	Film	Art

C Choose one of the famous people from the list. Don't tell your classmates. Make a list of five key points about the person.

1. _____
2. _____
3. _____
4. _____
5. _____

TIP

Speak slowly and clearly when you give a presentation.

D Stand up. Tell a group about your famous person. Don't say the person's name. Your classmates will guess the person.

PRESENT

I can... use lists to organize my ideas.   ☐ Very well   ☐ Well   ☐ Not very well

5 Food and drinks

Listening
Listening for a specific purpose

Speaking
Expressing likes and dislikes

Grammar
Simple present; Yes/No questions

Writing
Using a T-chart to organize ideas

Viewing
Connecting to the video

Presenting
Introducing your topic

1 VOCABULARY AND LISTENING

A Listen and repeat.
CD 1-28

APPETIZERS
Soup: $5.95
Salad: $5.50

ENTRÉES
Spaghetti: $9.95
Steak: $18.95
Chicken: $13.50
Fish: $14.75

SIDES
Carrots: $1.50
French fries: $2.75

DESSERTS
Cake: $4.50
Pie: $4.25

DRINKS
Coffee: $2.50
Tea: $2.00

B Check ✓ the items that don't belong.

1. **Sides**   ☐ cake   ☐ carrots   ☐ French fries
2. **Drinks**   ☐ tea   ☑ salad   ☐ coffee
3. **Appetizers**   ☑ fish   ☐ soup   ☐ salad
4. **Entrées**   ☐ steak   ☐ chicken   ☐ pie
5. **Desserts**   ☐ cake   ☐ pie   ☐ chicken

> **LISTENING**
> **Listening for a specific purpose**
> You always have a purpose for listening. For example, you can listen to identify a decision someone makes.

C Listen to a woman in a restaurant. What does the woman NOT order? Circle the correct answer.
CD 1-29

a. an appetizer   b. an entrée   c. a side   d. a drink   e. a dessert

D *Listen Again* Circle the picture of the woman's meal.
CD 1-29

1.   2.   3.

I can... listen for a specific purpose.   ☐ Very well   ☐ Well   ☐ Not very well

2 SPEAKING

A Complete the conversation with the phrases from the box.

is really good	Jay Street	I love it	are great

A: Do you like Mexican food? B: Oh, yes, __I love it__!
A: What's a good Mexican restaurant? B: Mia's Mexican Kitchen __are great__.
A: Do they have tacos? B: Yes, the tacos __is really good__.
A: Where is it? B: It's on __Jay Street__.

B Listen to the conversation. Then practice with a partner.
CD 1-30

Amy: Do you like Italian food?
Patrick: Oh, yes. I love it!
Amy: I do, too. Luigi's is my favorite Italian restaurant.
Patrick: Do they have pizza?
Amy: Oh, yeah. The pizza is great. And the spaghetti's good, too.
Patrick: Where is it?
Amy: It's on Prince Street.
Patrick: OK. Let's go! I'm hungry!

SPEAKING
Expressing likes and dislikes

Use *like*, *love*, and *hate* to express likes and dislikes: I like pizza. I love Japanese food. I hate onions!

ONLINE PRACTICE

C Work in pairs. Practice the conversation below with your own information.

A: I like _____ food.
B: I do, too. What's your favorite _____ restaurant?
A: _____ is my favorite. What's your favorite _____ restaurant?
B: I love _____.

D **Pronunciation** Stressing opinions Notice the word stress in these sentences.
CD 1-31

1. I **like** it.
2. I **love** pizza.
3. I **hate** onions.
4. This restaurant is **great**.

CULTURE TALK!

In Japan, people don't usually eat dessert after a meal. What do you eat at the end of a meal?

I can... express likes and dislikes. ☐ Very well ☐ Well ☐ Not very well

UNIT 5   29

3 GRAMMAR

A Listen. Then listen again and repeat.

Grammar Reference page 86

Simple present: affirmative and negative statements; Yes/No questions		
I **like** chicken. You **like** coffee.	I **don't like** fish. You **don't like** tea.	**Do** you **like** chicken? Yes, I **do**. / No, I **don't**.
He **likes** chicken.	She **doesn't like** steak.	**Does** he **like** steak? Yes, he **does**. / No, he **doesn't**.
We **like** cake.	We **don't like** pie.	**Do** they **like** desserts? Yes, they **do**. / No, they **don't**.

B Complete each sentence with the correct form of the verb in parentheses.

1. Sam __love__ pizza. (love)
2. He __doesn't live__ spaghetti. (not like)
3. __Do__ you __eat__ a salad every day? (eat)
4. I __don't eat__ dessert. (not eat)
5. __Do__ Sam and Alex __like__ Mexican food? (like)

C Work in pairs. Ask questions and give answers. Use the simple present.

Example:
Anna / like / spaghetti
A: Does Anna like spaghetti?
B: No, she doesn't.

1. Sarah / like / cake
2. Mike / like / carrots 
3. you / like / pie 
4. your friends / like / fish 
5. your mother / like / tea 
6. Sandra / like / coffee 

D Grammar Talk! Does he like Chinese food? Student A page 96, Student B page 99.

I can... use the simple present. ☐ Very well ☐ Well ☐ Not very well

30

4 READING AND WRITING

A Read and listen. When do you use this kind of website?

Chico's Restaurant
52 reviews for Chico's Restaurant

Millie F
Chico's is my favorite restaurant. I love the food. It's not cheap, but the hamburgers are great!
Food: ★★★★★   Prices: ★★★

Philip K
The food is good, but it is expensive. I like the sandwiches, and I love the French fries. I don't like the spaghetti.
Food: ★★★★   Prices: ★

Ramona J
I like Chico's Restaurant. The chicken is great. The desserts are delicious. The apple pie is my favorite. I don't like the fish. The coffee is also bad.
Food: ★★   Prices: ★★

B Read again. Complete the T-chart. Do you want to go to Chico's?

Good things about Chico's	Bad things about Chico's
hamburgers	

> **WRITING**
> **Using a T-chart**
> Use a T-chart to organize your ideas and show two sides of a topic, like good things or bad things.
>
> ONLINE PRACTICE

C Think of a restaurant in your town. List good and bad things about it.

Good things about _____	Bad things about _____

D Write a review of the restaurant from Part C.

I like / don't like _____. The _____ are good.
The _____ are bad. I love the _____. I don't like the _____.

I can... use a T-chart to organize ideas.   ☐ Very well   ☐ Well   ☐ Not very well

UNIT 5   31

5 VIEWING: Hong Kong food tour

A Look at the picture and map. Where is this restaurant? What kind of food do you think the people are eating?

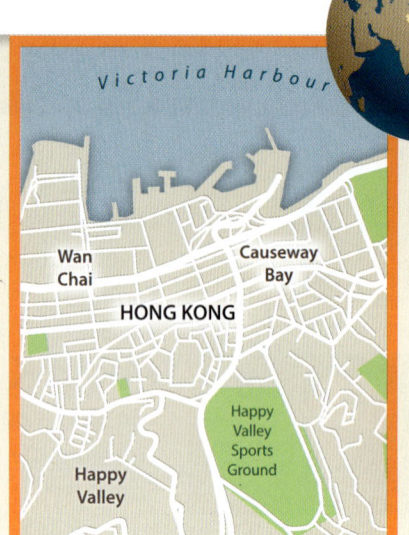

B Watch the video. Check ✓ the things Fiona does in Hong Kong. What do *you* do when you visit a city? Circle the things.

- ☐ goes to a market
- ☐ goes to an amusement park
- ☐ sees a friend
- ☐ eats at a food court
- ☐ takes photos
- ☐ eats at a restaurant
- ☐ works at a restaurant
- ☐ goes to a museum

> **VIEWING**
> **Connecting to the video**
> How does the video connect to your life? Think about how you are similar to the people in the video.
>
> ONLINE PRACTICE

C Read the questions. Then watch again and circle *Yes* or *No*. Ask and answer the questions with a partner.

1. Do some people in Hong Kong eat five meals every day?   Yes   No
2. Does the Causeway Bay Market sell Japanese food?   Yes   No
3. Is Walter a food critic?   Yes   No
4. Is the food court expensive?   Yes   No
5. Is the restaurant famous?   Yes   No
6. Does Fiona like dim sum?   Yes   No

D Complete the chart with places in your city. Then talk about your ideas with a small group.

Kind of place	Name of the place
A good food court	
A famous restaurant	
A big market	

I can... connect to a video.   ☐ Very well   ☐ Well   ☐ Not very well

6 PRESENTING

A Read the presentation. Underline the introduction. What three things does the introduction talk about? Write them below.

_____   _____   _____

PRESENTING
Introducing your topic
First, introduce your topic – tell your audience what your presentation is about. This helps people follow your presentation.

ONLINE PRACTICE

> My presentation today is about three good restaurants in this city – a cheap restaurant, an expensive restaurant, and a fun restaurant.
>
> The cheap restaurant is Joe's Pizza. They have really good pizza, and the servers are friendly.
>
> The expensive restaurant is The Villa. It's a small restaurant in a beautiful old house. They have wonderful Italian food. My favorite dish there is the spaghetti with tomato sauce. For dessert, their chocolate cake is delicious.
>
> The fun restaurant is Fire and Ice. They have live music there every night. Their tacos are great.

B Think of three good restaurants in your city. What are three good things about each one? Make notes in the chart.

Cheap restaurant	Expensive restaurant	Fun restaurant
1.	1.	1.
2.	2.	2.
3.	3.	3.

TIP
Pause (stop for a moment) between your descriptions of each restaurant.

C Stand up. Use your notes from Part B to tell a group about your restaurants. Remember to introduce your topic.

PRESENT

> **I can...** introduce my topic.   ☐ Very well   ☐ Well   ☐ Not very well

6 Things we do

Listening
Making guesses

Speaking
Adding information (1)

Grammar
Present continuous; Yes/No questions

Reading
Making guesses

Viewing
Taking notes

Presenting
Ending a presentation

1 VOCABULARY AND LISTENING

A Listen and repeat.
CD 1-34

1. sleeping
2. studying 
3. shopping 
4. cooking dinner 
5. going to work 
6. taking a shower 
7. texting 
8. talking on the phone 

B Complete the chart with words or phrases from Part A. Different answers are possible.

Things you usually do at home	Things you usually do away from home
I usually study at home.	I usually shoop away from home.
I usually sleep at home.	I usually going to work away from home.
I usually cook dinner at home.	
I usually take a shower at home.	
I usually text at home from home.	

> **LISTENING**
> **Making guesses**
> When we listen, we make guesses about things that a speaker does not say. For example, *I'm studying* indicates the speaker is a student.
>
> ONLINE PRACTICE

C Listen to people talking about activities.
CD 1-35 Number the pictures from *1–4*.

a.   b.    c.    d.

D Listen Again Make guesses about the statements. Circle the correct answers.
CD 1-35
1. a. Ana needs new clothes.
   b. Ana doesn't have money.
2. a. The baby's hungry.
   b. The baby's tired.
3. a. It's evening.
   b. It's morning.
4. a. Pam is a student.
   b. Pam is a teacher.

I can... make guesses about everyday activities. ☐ Very well ☐ Well ☐ Not very well

34

2 SPEAKING

A Match the questions and answers.

- c 1. Hello?
- d 2. Where are you?
- b 3. Are you at work?
- a 4. What are you doing?

a. I'm going to class.
b. No, I'm not.
c. Hi, Kate. It's Linda.
d. I'm at home.

B Listen to the conversation. Then practice with a partner.
CD 1-36

Sana: Hello?
Nick: Hi, Sana. It's me, Nick.
Sana: Oh, hi, Nick.
Nick: Where are you? Are you at home?
Sana: No, I'm not. **I'm exercising.** Where are you?
Nick: I'm at home. **I'm cooking dinner.** Are you hungry?
Sana: Yeah, I'm really hungry!

SPEAKING
Adding information (1)
Do not answer a question with only one word. Add information like the sentences in red to keep the conversation going.

ONLINE PRACTICE

C **Pronunciation** Linking Listen and repeat. We usually link the same consonants when they are next to each other.
CD 1-37

1. She isn't texting. *(is not)*
2. She's sleeping.
3. They're reading. *(Are)*

D Work in pairs. Practice the conversation below with your own information.

A: Hello?
B: Hi, __Marian__. It's me, __Elvis__.
A: Oh, hi, __Elvis__.
B: Where are you? Are you at home?
A: No, I'm not. I'm __shopping__. Where are you?
B: I'm __studying__.

I can... add information.   ☐ Very well   ☐ Well   ☐ Not very well

UNIT 6   35

3 GRAMMAR

A Listen. Then listen again and repeat.

Grammar Reference page 87

Present continuous: affirmative and negative statements; Yes/No questions		
I**'m studying**.	I**'m not working**.	**Are** you **working**?
		Yes, I **am**. / No, I**'m not**.
He**'s reading**.	He **isn't speaking**.	**Is** he **texting**?
She**'s texting**.	She **isn't talking** on the phone.	Yes, he **is**. / No, he **isn't**.
You**'re cooking** dinner.	You **aren't eating** lunch.	**Are** you **eating** dinner?
They**'re sleeping**.	They **aren't studying**.	Yes, we **are**. / No, we **aren't**.

B Complete each sentence with the correct form of the verb in parentheses.

1. Ann __is cooking__ ¹ dinner. (cook) She _____² lunch. (not cook)
2. We _____³ (study). We _____⁴ (not sleep).
3. I _____⁵ on the phone. (not talk) I _____⁶ (text).
4. _____⁷ you _____⁸ to work? (go)
5. James _____⁹ right now. (sleep)

C Work in pairs. Ask questions and give answers.

Example:
Kim / shopping
A: Is Kim shopping?
B: Yes, she is.

Example:
Andy / studying
A: Is Andy studying?
B: No, he isn't. He's cooking.

1. Marco / studying
2. Robert / texting 
3. Jen and Cathy / studying 
4. Julia / taking a shower 
5. Kim and Pedro / talking on the phone 
6. Maria / sleeping 

D Grammar Talk! **Is he sleeping?** Student A page 96, Student B page 99.

I can... ask and answer present continuous *Yes/No* questions.   ☐ Very well   ☐ Well   ☐ Not very well

36

4 READING AND WRITING

A Read and listen. What are the women texting about?

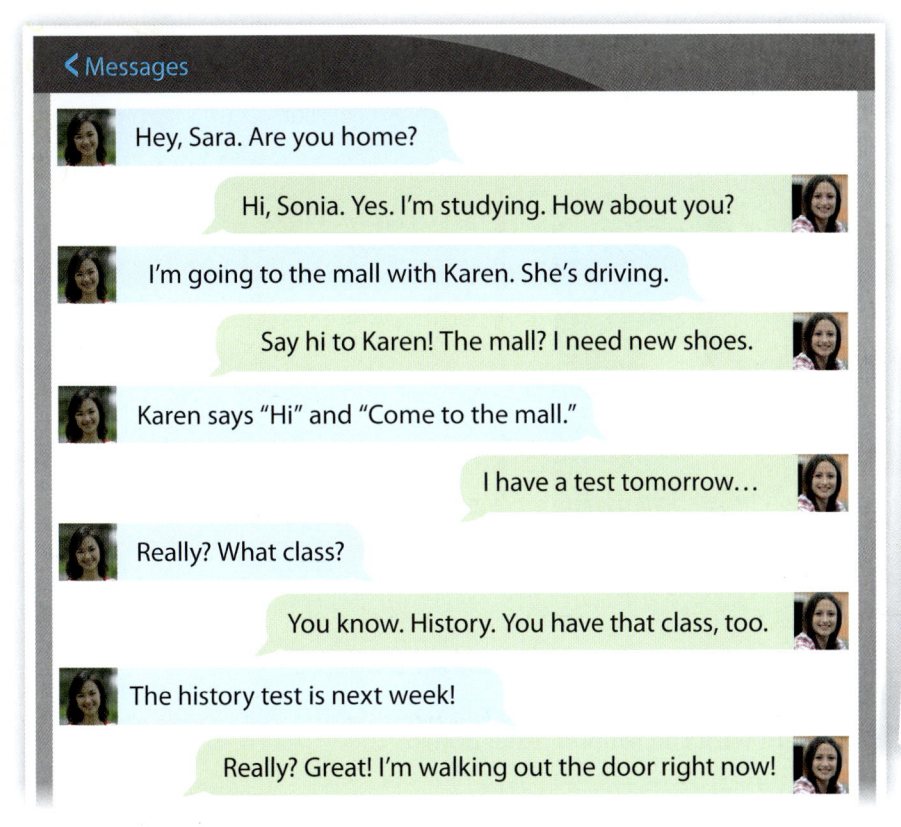

> **Messages**
>
> Hey, Sara. Are you home?
>
> Hi, Sonia. Yes. I'm studying. How about you?
>
> I'm going to the mall with Karen. She's driving.
>
> Say hi to Karen! The mall? I need new shoes.
>
> Karen says "Hi" and "Come to the mall."
>
> I have a test tomorrow…
>
> Really? What class?
>
> You know. History. You have that class, too.
>
> The history test is next week!
>
> Really? Great! I'm walking out the door right now!

READING
Making guesses
You can make guesses when you read. Look for clues that tell you more about the writer and the topic.

ONLINE PRACTICE

B Read again. Write **T** (true) or **F** (false) next to the sentences. Correct the false sentences.

___ 1. Sara is a student.
___ 2. Sara is studying.
___ 3. Sonia is a student.
___ 4. Sara doesn't know Karen.
___ 5. Sara and Sonia have a history test tomorrow.

C Who do you text? What do you text about? Complete the information.

People I text: _____ _____ _____

What I text about: _____ _____ _____

D Complete the texting conversation. Use your own ideas.

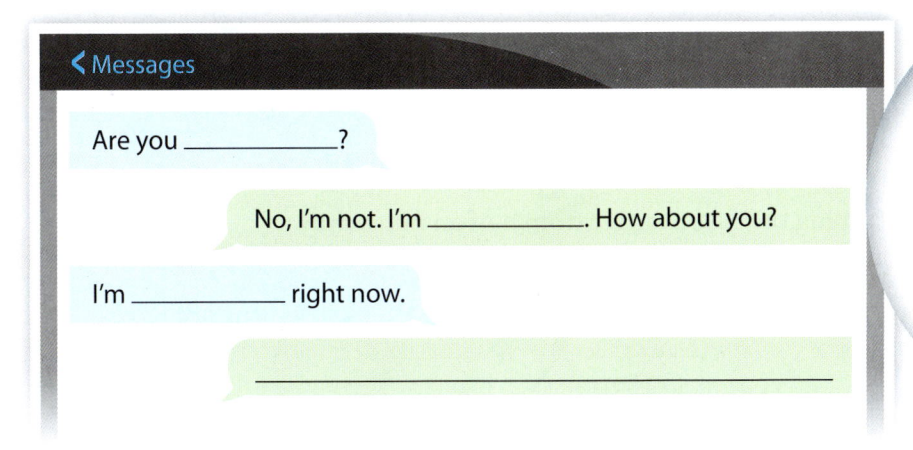

> **Messages**
>
> Are you _____?
>
> No, I'm not. I'm _____. How about you?
>
> I'm _____ right now.
>
> _____

CULTURE TALK!

China is the number one country for texting. Chinese phone users send about 71 billion texts a month. How often do you text?

I can... make guesses when I read. ☐ Very well ☐ Well ☐ Not very well

UNIT 6 37

5 VIEWING: Robot doctors

A Look at the picture. Find a doctor, a patient, a robot, a nurse. Why do you think the robot is in the hospital?

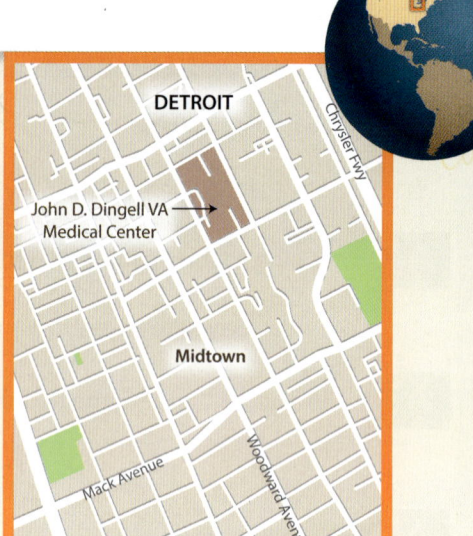

B Watch the video. What are some good things about robot doctors? What is one problem with the robots? Take notes.

Good things	One problem

**VIEWING
Taking notes**
Take notes as you watch. Just write words, not sentences. This helps you remember important information.

ONLINE PRACTICE

C Watch again. Complete the sentences. Use words from the box.

| robot | power | home | doctors | patients | medicine ✓ |

1. The robots are helping to improve __medicine__.
2. Doctors can be at _____ and in the hospital at the same time.
3. Dr. Santucci is controlling the _____ from half an hour away.
4. The _____ and the _____ like the robots.
5. There is just one problem with the robots – they need _____.

D Work with a partner. Discuss the questions.

1. Do you think robot doctors are a good idea? Why or why not?
2. What other jobs do robots do?

I can... take notes as I watch.   ☐ Very well   ☐ Well   ☐ Not very well

6 PRESENTING

A Read and listen to the information in the blog. Complete the summary at the end with the correct words. How many ideas are in the summary?

PRESENTING
Ending a presentation
At the end of your presentation, summarize your ideas in one sentence. This helps your audience remember your important points.

ONLINE PRACTICE

MY MORNING ROUTINE

On weekday mornings, I usually get up at 6:00. I check my texts, and then I go for a walk in the park. After that I take a shower. At about 7:30 I have breakfast, usually toast and coffee. At 8:00 I take the subway to work. I start work at 9:00. So that's my morning: texts, a _____, a shower, _____, and work.

B Make notes about your morning routine. On weekday mornings, I:

- _____
- _____
- _____
- _____

C Write an ending for your presentation. Summarize your ideas in one sentence.

So that's my morning:
_____
_____

TIP
Stress the times. For example, say six o'clock more loudly.

D Stand up. Use your notes from Part B and Part C to tell a group about your morning routine.

I can... end my presentation with a summary. ☐ Very well ☐ Well ☐ Not very well

39

Self-Assessment

1 VOCABULARY

Circle the correct word or words to complete each sentence.

1. Mark has blond hair / eyes / height. He's tall.
2. Susan has blue hair / eyes / height. Her hair is brown.
3. Alex is average tall / short / height. He has brown eyes.

I can... understand descriptions of people.
(Unit 4)

4. A: Can I get you a drink?
   B: Yes. A salad / pie / coffee, please.
5. A: How about an appetizer?
   B: Spaghetti / Pie / Soup, please.
6. A: And for your entrée?
   B: Carrots / Steak / Tea, please.

I can... understand vocabulary about food.
(Unit 5)

7. David is in his bedroom. He's cooking dinner / sleeping / taking a shower.
8. We're at the mall. We're studying / shopping / cooking dinner.
9. I'm working / studying / texting. I have a test tonight.
10. Please be quiet. Mom is taking a shower / going to work / talking on the phone.

I can... understand vocabulary about everyday activities.
(Unit 6)

2 GRAMMAR

1. Jackie have / has / haves brown hair.
2. I have / has / haves green eyes.
3. They doesn't have / don't has / don't have black hair.

I can... ask and answer Yes/No questions with have.
(Unit 4)

4. Sam love / loves / loving pizza.
5. I don't like / doesn't like / not like fish.
6. Does Joe like / Do Joe like / Do Joe likes coffee?

I can... ask and answer simple present Yes/No questions.
(Unit 5)

7. Max and Lisa are eating / is eating / am eating lunch.
8. Ken aren't / am not / isn't going to work today.
9. Are you / Is you / You aren't studying right now?
10. Are Luke / Luke's / Is Luke sleeping?

I can... ask and answer present continuous Yes/No questions.
(Unit 6)

Units 4-6

3 READING

A Read and listen. Who is making dinner?

Brian Jones

Are you hungry? Come over to our house! Paul and I are cooking dinner right now. I'm making spaghetti. Paul's making salad. We have drinks here. You can bring dessert.

Profile
Photos (51)
Notes
Friends

LIKE | COMMENT | SHARE | 2 HOURS AGO

John Silva: Hey, Brian. I'm very hungry! I love spaghetti. I can bring dessert. I have some apple pie. My friend Robert can't come. He's studying. He has a test tomorrow. What time is dinner?!

B Match the people on the left with the sentence endings on the right.

___ 1. Brian and Paul   a. is making spaghetti.
___ 2. Brian   b. is hungry.
___ 3. Paul   c. is making salad.
___ 4. John   d. is studying.
___ 5. Robert   e. are cooking dinner.

C Read the statements. Write **T** (true) or **F** (false). Correct the false statements.

___ 1. Brian is making apple pie.
___ 2. Brian and Paul don't have drinks.
___ 3. John doesn't like spaghetti.
___ 4. John has a test tomorrow.
___ 5. Robert is Paul's friend.

D What three foods do you love? What are three foods that you don't like?

I love _____, _____, and _____.
I don't like _____, _____, and _____.

SELF-ASSESSMENT | UNITS 4-6   41

7 At home

Listening
Using visuals
Speaking
Explaining your reasons

Grammar
There is/There are; prepositions of place
Writing
Writing a topic sentence

Viewing
Identifying facts and opinions
Presentation
Using visuals

1 VOCABULARY AND LISTENING

A Listen and repeat.
CD 2-01

1. living room
2. dining room
3. kitchen
4. bedroom
5. bathroom
6. yard
7. garage
8. hall
9. closet
10. balcony
11. stairs

B Match the descriptions of the rooms with the rooms.

_b_ 1. You eat in this room.   a. living room
_e_ 2. You sleep in this room.   b. dining room
_d_ 3. You take a shower in this room. c. kitchen
_c_ 4. You cook in this room.   d. bathroom
_a_ 5. You watch TV in this room.   e. bedroom

C Listen to people talking about their apartments. Number the pictures from 1–3.
CD 2-02

a. 2   b. 1   c. 3

LISTENING
Using visuals
Visuals (pictures) offer great support when you listen. Look at small differences between the pictures to identify the correct answers.

ONLINE PRACTICE

D Listen Again Do the people like their apartments? Write Yes or No.
CD 2-02

1. Zai _Yes_   2. Jessica _Yes_   3. Jake _No_

▶ **I can...** use visuals to listen about housing.   ☐ Very well   ☐ Well   ☐ Not very well

42

2 SPEAKING

A Put the conversation in the correct order. Number the sentences from 1–6.

_5_ Are the bedrooms large?
_4_ There are two.
_1_ Do you like your new apartment, Kim?
_3_ Is there one bedroom or two?
_2_ I love it.
_6_ Yes, they're really big.

B Listen to the conversation. Then practice with a partner.
CD 2-03

Mika: Oh, I like your apartment, Daisy. It's really nice.
Daisy: Thanks. I like it because it's big.
Mika: Does it have one bedroom or two?
Daisy: It has two. And there's a living room, a kitchen, and a big bathroom.
Mika: Nice. Does it have a lot of closets?
Daisy: Yes, there are four big closets.
Mika: That's great!

SPEAKING
Explaining your reasons
Use *because* to explain your reasons. Use a subject and verb after *because*.

ONLINE PRACTICE

C Work in pairs. Practice the conversation below with your own information.

A: Tell me about your apartment.
B: Well, it has a __kitchen__, a __bedroom__, and a __2 bathroom__.
A: Do you like it?
B: Yes. I like it because __is a big__. / No, I don't like it because __isn't yard__.

D Pronunciation Word stress Listen and repeat. We stress the first syllable in most two-syllable nouns.
CD 2-04

1. **clos**et   2. **kitch**en   3. **bed**room   4. **bath**room   5. **show**er

> **I can...** explain my reasons. ☐ Very well ☐ Well ☐ Not very well

UNIT 7 43

3 GRAMMAR

A Listen. Then listen again and repeat.

Grammar Reference page 88

There is/There are; Yes/No questions; prepositions of place	
There's a bathroom on the second floor.	**There are** some closets in the bedroom.
There's no bathroom on the first floor.	**There are** no closets in the hall.
There isn't a bathroom on the first floor.	**There aren't** any closets in the hall.
Is there a yard?	Yes, **there is**. / No, **there isn't**.
Are there any closets?	Yes, **there are**. / No, **there aren't**.
NOTE: **in** the bedroom **in** the kitchen **on** the second floor **on** the first floor	

B Complete each sentence with *There is, There are, Is there,* or *Are there* and *in* or *on*.

1. ___There Are___ three bedrooms ___in___ the apartment.
2. ___There is___ a bathroom ___on___ the second floor.
3. ___Are There___ any closets ___on___ the first floor?
4. ___There is___ no closet ___in___ the bathroom.
5. ___Is there___ a dining room ___in___ the apartment?

C Work in pairs. Ask questions and give answers.

Example:
a living room
A: Is there a living room?
B: Yes, there is.

1. a bathroom
2. a shower in the bathroom 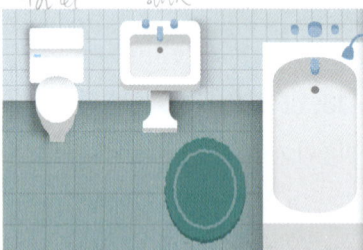
3. two bedrooms 
4. two closets in the bedroom 
5. a yard 
6. a second floor 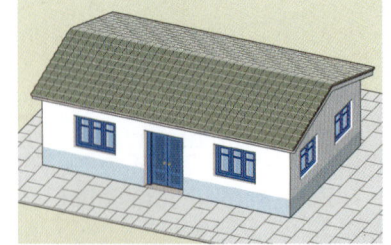

D Grammar Talk! Is there a yard? Student A page 100, Student B page 103.

I can... use *there is/there are* and prepositions of place.   ☐ Very well   ☐ Well   ☐ Not very well

44

4 READING AND WRITING

A Read and listen to the article. What do the houses have in common?

Strange Houses

Most houses look alike. They have four walls and a ceiling. They have one or more bedrooms and one or more bathrooms. Some houses are small, and some houses are big, but they are not very different. However, there are a few very strange houses in the world.

Three strange houses don't look like houses at all. The Bubble House near Cannes, France, looks like a bubble! It is very large. There are 28 round rooms in the house. There are ten bedrooms. The Shoe House in Hellam, Pennsylvania, is also unusual. It looks like a giant shoe. But it is not very big. It has three bedrooms, two bathrooms, and a living room. There is also a kitchen. The One-Log House in Garberville, California, looks like a tree. That's because it is made from a single tree! It is very big, but there is only one bedroom in it.

B Read again. Complete the sentences.
1. The Bubble House has __28__ rooms.
2. There are __ten__ bedrooms in the Bubble House.
3. There are __two__ bathrooms in the Shoe House.
4. The __Shoe__ House has a living room.
5. The __One Log house__ has one bedroom.

C Underline the topic sentences in the article.

WRITING
Writing a topic sentence
Use a topic sentence to introduce the main idea of the paragraph and tell your reader what it is about.

ONLINE PRACTICE

D Complete the chart about a home you know.

Is the house big or small?	Rooms	How many?

E Write a paragraph about a house you know. Use the notes from Part D. Start with a topic sentence.

I can... write a topic sentence. ☐ Very well ☐ Well ☐ Not very well

UNIT 7 45

5 VIEWING: Tiny houses

A Look at the photo. What is unusual about this house?

B Watch the video. Are these statements facts or opinions? Write **F** (fact) or **O** (opinion).

F 1. "Tiny houses are becoming more popular these days."
F 2. "There's a closet and some shelves."
O 3. "I think they're amazing."
O 4. "Nice house!"
F 5. "There's one bathroom with a shower."
O 6. "Tiny houses are a great way to have a simple and inexpensive life."

> **VIEWING**
> **Identifying facts and opinions**
> Try to identify facts (true things), and opinions (things a person believes). People sometimes say *I think* before opinions.
>
> ONLINE PRACTICE

C Watch again. For each house, circle the statement that *isn't* true.

House #1	House #2	House #3
a. It has wheels.	a. It is very narrow.	a. There are small windows.
b. It has two tiny bedrooms.	b. It has an indoor garden.	b. There aren't any closets.
c. There's a closet.	c. There isn't a shower.	c. The table doesn't have legs.

D What are the pros (good things) and cons (bad things) of tiny houses? Make notes in the chart. Then talk about your ideas with a partner.

Pros (good things)	Cons (bad things)

I can... identify facts and opinions. ☐ Very well ☐ Well ☐ Not very well

6 PRESENTING

A Look at the picture. What words do you think are in the presentation about the house? Write them below.

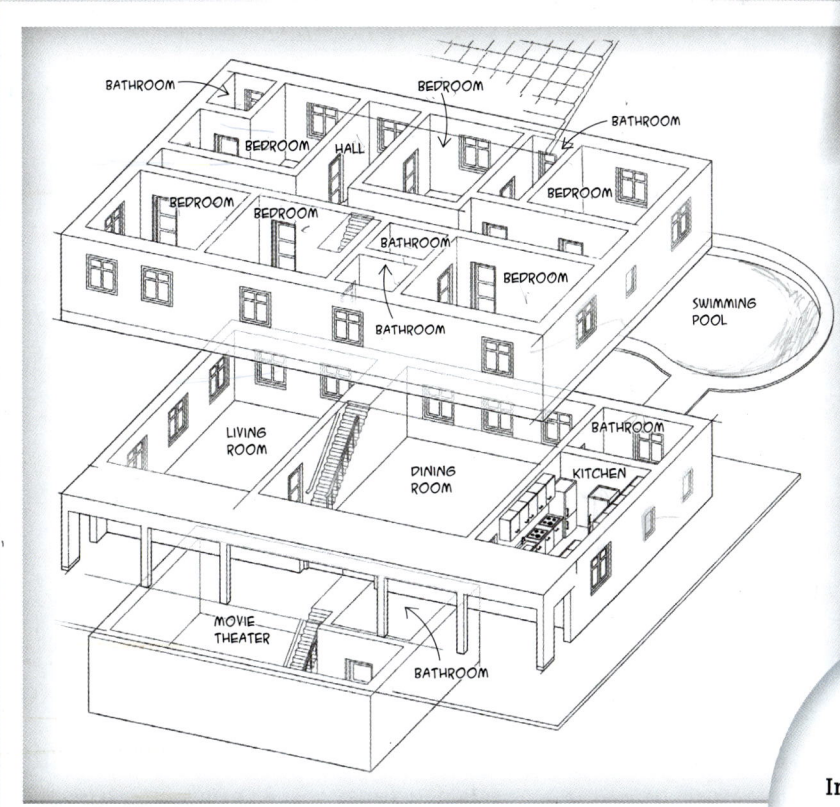

**PRESENTING
Using visuals**
Use visuals – photos, illustrations, sketches, drawings. They help make your presentation clear and easy to follow.

ONLINE PRACTICE

1. The house has a swimming pool.
2. The house has six bedroom in the second floor.
3. The house has a dining room in the first floor and is very spacious.
4. The house has a movie theater in the cellar.
5. _____
6. _____

CULTURE TALK!

In the U.S., buildings don't have the 13th floor because 13 is an unlucky number. What numbers are unlucky in your country?

B Listen to the presentation. Circle the words from Part A that you hear.
CD 2-07

C Draw a picture of your dream house. You can draw it on paper or on a computer. Think about these questions:

1. Where is it?
2. How many floors does it have?
3. How many rooms does it have?
4. What else does it have?

TIP
Point to your visual when you are presenting.

D Stand up. Tell a group about your dream house. Point to your picture as you talk.
PRESENT

I can... use visuals when I give a presentation. ☐ Very well ☐ Well ☐ Not very well

47

8 Free time activities

Listening
Listening for tone (1)

Speaking
Showing interest

Grammar
Simple present: Wh- questions

Reading
Identifying a writer's purpose

Viewing
Paying attention to numbers

Presenting
Using charts and graphs

1 VOCABULARY AND LISTENING

A Listen and repeat.
CD 2-08

1. go to the movies
2. go shopping 
3. eat out 
4. work out at the gym 
5. watch TV 
6. listen to music 
7. play video games 
8. hang out with friends 

B Match the words to make phrases.

___ 1. listen to   a. shopping
___ 2. play   b. video games
___ 3. go to   c. TV
___ 4. go   d. music
___ 5. watch   e. the movies

> **LISTENING**
> **Listening for tone (1)**
> Tone tells you how a speaker feels. Tone shows if the speakers are happy or sad, or if they like or don't like something.
>
> ONLINE PRACTICE

C Circle the activities that the speakers are talking about.
CD 2-09

1. a. watching TV   b. playing video games   c. going to the movies
2. a. eating out   b. working out   c. listening to music
3. a. playing video games   b. watching TV   c. going shopping
4. a. playing video games   b. going to the movies   c. hanging out with friends

D *Listen Again* Do the speakers like the activities? Check ✓ *Yes* or *No*.
CD 2-09

1. ☐ Yes ☐ No
2. ☐ Yes ☐ No
3. ☐ Yes ☐ No
4. ☐ Yes ☐ No

I can... listen for tone about free time activities.   ☐ Very well   ☐ Well   ☐ Not very well

2 SPEAKING

A Complete the conversation with the sentences from the box.

> Oh, I like video games, too.   I go to the movies.   No, I go with friends. How about you?

A: What do you do in your free time?   B: _____

A: Do you go to the movies alone?   B: _____

A: I play video games.   B: _____

B Listen to the conversation. Then practice with a partner.
CD 2-10

Sabrina: So, what do you do in your free time?
Carmen: Well, I go shopping a lot.
Sabrina: Oh? Where?
Carmen: Anywhere. Big department stores, small stores . . . I just love to go shopping.
Sabrina: That's interesting. Do you go shopping every day?
Carmen: No, I don't go every day. I go once a week.
Sabrina: Who do you go with?
Carmen: Usually with my sister and my friend.

> **SPEAKING**
> **Showing interest**
> You can use *Oh?* and *That's interesting* to show interest in what someone is saying.
>
> ONLINE PRACTICE

C Work in pairs. Practice the conversation below with your own information.

A: So, what do you do in your free time?   B: I _go shopping_.
A: Oh? Do you _go shopping_ every day?   B: _yes, I do_. How about you?
A: I _go to the movie_   B: Do you _____ a lot?
A: _yes, I do_.   B: That's interesting.

D **Pronunciation** **Reductions** Listen and repeat. *What do you* can
CD 2-11   sometimes sound like one word.

1. **What do you** do on weekends?
2. **What do you** do with your friends?
3. **What do you** do in the evenings?
4. **What do you** do with your family?

I can... show interest.   ☐ Very well   ☐ Well   ☐ Not very well

UNIT 8   49

3 GRAMMAR

A Listen. Then listen again and repeat.

Grammar Reference page 89

Simple present: Wh- questions	
What do you **do** in your free time?	I work out.
Where do you **work out**?	At a gym.
How often does Ken **play** video games?	Every night.
Who does Claire **hang out** with?	Her friends.
When do we **go shopping**?	On the weekend.
How often do they **watch TV**?	Never.

B Complete each question with a Wh- word + do/does.

1. A: _____ you do on weekends?   B: I go shopping.
2. A: _____ you go to the movies?   B: Twice a month.
3. A: _____ Karen go to shopping with?   B: Her friend Jung.
4. A: _____ they play video games?   B: On Friday nights.
5. A: _____ Andrew hang out with his friends?   B: At the mall.

C Work in pairs. Ask questions and give answers.

Example: you / at the mall
A: Where do you go shopping?
B: At the mall.

1. your friend / at home
2. your family / in the evenings 
3. Susan / with her sister 
4. they / once a month 
5. your neighbors / their friends 
6. you / every day 

D Grammar Talk! **What does he do on weekends?** Student A page 100, Student B page 103.

I can... ask Wh- questions in the simple present. ☐ Very well ☐ Well ☐ Not very well

50

4 READING AND WRITING

A Read and listen to the article. What is it about?

How often do you play video games?

Video games are popular all around the world, and people spend a lot of time playing them. How often do people play these games? Over 500 million people play video games and computer games every day.

These people play for an hour or more. About five million people in the United States play video games 40 hours a week. Every week, people around the world play video games and computer games for three billion hours.

B Read again. Complete the sentences with phrases from the box.

| an hour or more | every day | 40 hours a week | three billion hours a week | five million |

1. Half a billion people play video and computer games _____.
2. They play for _____.
3. In the United States, _____ people play a lot.
4. These people in the United States play _____.
5. Players all around the world play for _____.

C What is the writer's purpose in Part A?
   a. to entertain   b. to give information   c. to share an opinion

D Complete the chart about your free time activities.

Activity	How often?

> **READING**
> **Identifying a writer's purpose**
> When you read, ask *What is the writer's purpose?* To entertain? Give information? Share an opinion?
>
> ONLINE PRACTICE

E Complete the sentences. Use your own ideas.

I spend my free time a few different ways.

I really like to _____.
                (activity)

I _____ _____.
  (activity)   (how often?)

I also like to _____.
              (activity)

I _____ _____.
  (activity)   (how often?)

> **I can...** identify a writer's purpose.   ☐ Very well   ☐ Well   ☐ Not very well

UNIT 8

5 VIEWING: Chess capital of the world

A Look at the photos. Where are the people? What are they doing?

B Watch the video. Read the questions. Circle the correct answers.

1. What is the chess capital of the world?
   a. Washington Square Park in New York City
   b. Greenwich Village in New York City

2. How often do children go to chess camp in the summer?
   a. Twice a week.
   b. Every day.

3. What do children do at the chess camp?
   a. They play chess, eat pizza, and do homework.
   b. They play chess, eat pizza, and play in the fountain.

4. Why is Justice Williams famous?
   a. He is a great chess player.
   b. He is a movie star.

C Watch again. Circle the correct number.

1. Over *70 / 17* percent of the chess players in the United States live in New York.
2. Every year, the number of chess players in the United States grows by *200 / 100* percent.
3. Street chess is very popular at *five to seven / fifty-seven* parks and locations in New York.
4. There are *two / three* kinds of chess players in New York.
5. Justice Williams is *14 / 15* years old.
6. Justice started playing chess when he was *eight / nine* years old.

D Work in a small group. Discuss the questions.

1. What are some popular games in your country?
2. What is your favorite game? Why do you like it?
3. What game do you want to learn?

VIEWING
Paying attention to numbers
Pay attention to numbers. They tell you about important details.

ONLINE PRACTICE

CULTURE TALK!
In Russia, 43% of people play chess. Is chess popular in your country? Do you play chess?

I can... pay attention to numbers. ☐ Very well ☐ Well ☐ Not very well

52

6 PRESENTING

A Look at the chart. How often do the people in Emma's class go to the movies? Listen and complete the pie chart with the missing numbers.

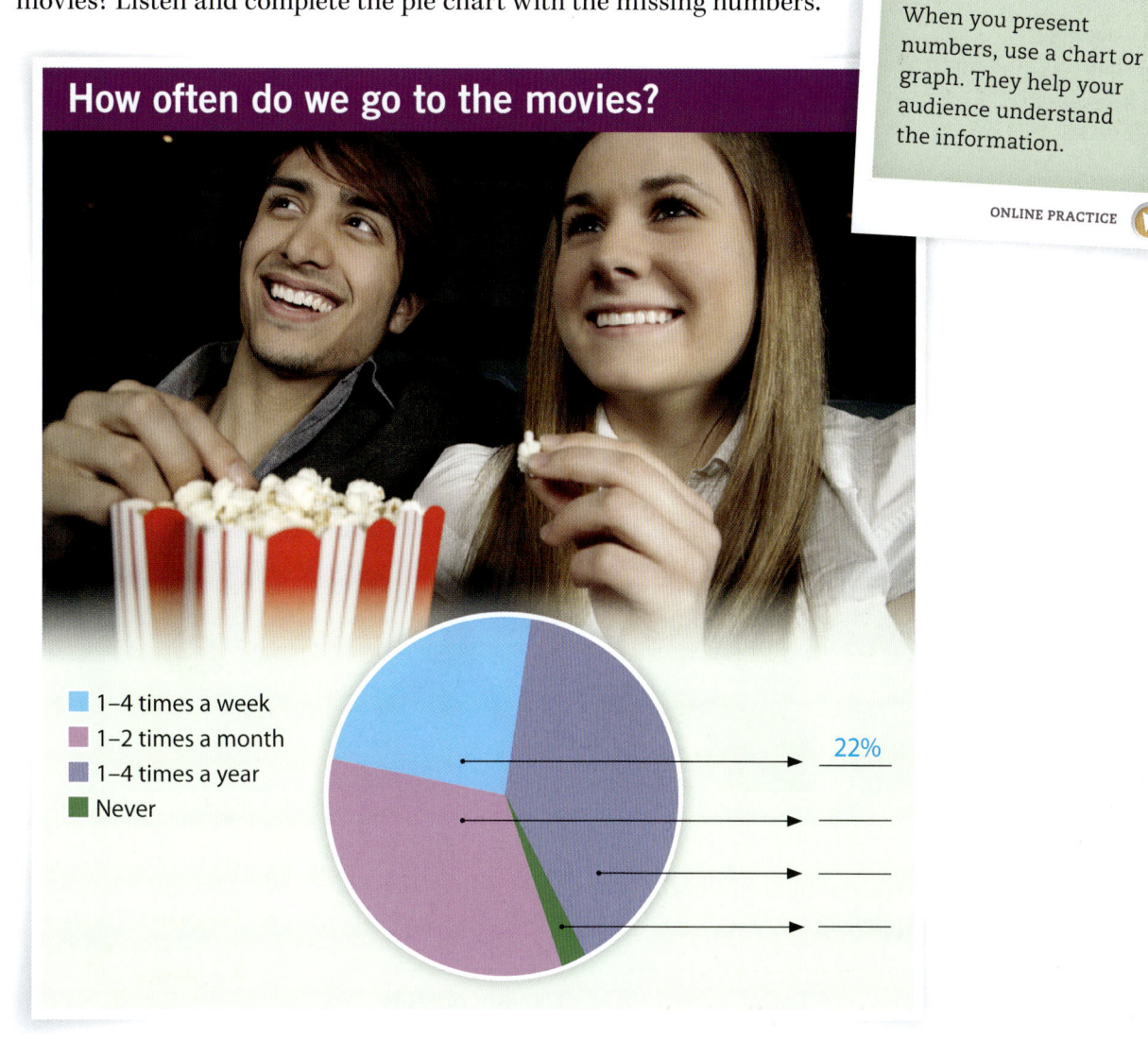

CD 2-14

> **PRESENTING**
> **Using charts and graphs**
> When you present numbers, use a chart or graph. They help your audience understand the information.
>
> ONLINE PRACTICE

How often do we go to the movies?

- 1–4 times a week
- 1–2 times a month
- 1–4 times a year
- Never

22%

B Choose a free time activity. Survey your classmates about how often they do the activity. Write the numbers in the chart below.

A: How often do you work out at the gym?   B: Twice a week.

Activity: _____

	1–4 times a week	1–2 times a month	1–4 times a year	Never
Number of students				

TIP
Point to your chart as you are presenting.

C Make a pie chart with the information from Part B. You can draw the chart or use a computer.

D Stand up. Tell your classmates about your survey. Show them your pie chart.

PRESENT

> **I can...** use charts and graphs in a presentation.   ☐ Very well   ☐ Well   ☐ Not very well

53

9 Popular sports

Listening
Listening for main ideas

Speaking
Adding information (2)

Grammar
Using *can* for ability

Writing
Using *and* and *but*

Viewing
Asking questions

Presenting
Supporting ideas with photos

1 VOCABULARY AND LISTENING

A Listen and repeat.
CD 2-15

1. play volleyball
2. play soccer 
3. play pool 
4. do martial arts 
5. do yoga 
6. go biking 
7. go snowboarding 
8. go swimming 

B Write the activities from Part A in the correct place in the chart. Add three new ideas.

Usually inside	Both	Usually outside

> **LISTENING**
> **Listening for main ideas**
> Listen for main ideas first. After you understand the main idea, you can understand details better.
>
> ONLINE PRACTICE

C Listen to people talking about sports. Match the people with the sports.
CD 2-16

___ 1. Tara   ___ 2. John   ___ 3. Jake   ___ 4. Rose   ___ 5. Dave

a. soccer   b. martial arts   c. swimming   d. biking   e. volleyball

D **Listen Again** How often do the people play or do the sports? Check ✓ the correct answer.
CD 2-16

	Every day	Once a week	Twice a week	Once a month	Never
1. Tara	☐	☐	☐	☐	☐
2. John	☐	☐	☐	☐	☐
3. Jake	☐	☐	☐	☐	☐
4. Rose	☐	☐	☐	☐	☐
5. Dave	☐	☐	☐	☐	☐

> **I can...** identify sports in conversations.   ☐ Very well   ☐ Well   ☐ Not very well

2 SPEAKING

A Put the conversation in order. Number the sentences from *1–5*.

___ Yes, swimming is my favorite sport.

___ I like volleyball and biking.

___ No, I can't swim. What about you?

_1_ What sports do you like?

___ Yeah, me too. Do you like swimming?

B Listen to the conversation. Then practice with a partner.

CD 2-17

SPEAKING
Adding information (2)
After a negative answer, add information to keep the conversation going. You sound more polite if you add information.

ONLINE PRACTICE

Jake: What sports do you like?
Brian: I like basketball and tennis.
Jake: Yeah, me, too. Can you play tennis?
Brian: No, I can't, **but I like to watch it on TV**. What about you? What sports do you like?
Eric: I like swimming and snowboarding.
Brian: Oh, really? Do you go snowboarding often?
Eric: Yes, I go snowboarding every winter.

C Work in pairs. Practice the conversation below with your own information.

A: Do you like biking?
B: No, I don't, but I like _____ and _____.
   What sports do you like?
A: I like _____ and _____.
B: How often do you _____?
A: _____.

CULTURE TALK!

Soccer and tennis are the two most popular sports in the world. What sports are popular in your country?

I can... add information after a negative answer. ☐ Very well ☐ Well ☐ Not very well

3 GRAMMAR

A Listen. Then listen again and repeat.

Grammar Reference page 90

Using *can* for ability		
I **can** play pool.	I **can't** play tennis.	**Can** you play soccer? Yes, I **can**. / No, I **can't**.
He **can** speak Chinese.	He **can't** speak Korean.	**Can** he speak French? Yes, he **can**. / No, he **can't**.
They **can** play volleyball well.	They **can't** do martial arts.	**Can** they swim? Yes, they **can**. / No, they **can't**.

B Write questions using *can* and the verbs in parentheses. Then write true short answers.

1. A: _____ you _____ ? (swim)   B: _____ , I _____ .
2. A: _____ you _____ ? (play soccer)   B: _____ , I _____ .
3. A: _____ you _____ ? (do martial arts)   B: _____ , I _____ .
4. A: _____ you _____ ? (snowboard)   B: _____ , I _____ .
5. A: _____ you _____ ? (do yoga)   B: _____ , I _____ .

C **Pronunciation** *Can* vs. *can't* Listen and repeat. *Can* often sounds like *kin* in statements and questions. In short answers and negative statements, we clearly pronounce the *a*.

I **can** ski.   **Can** you ski?   Yes, I **can**.   No, I **can't**.   I **can't** ski.

D Work in pairs. Ask questions and give answers.

Example: Tom / cook
A: Can Tom cook?
B: Yes, he can.

1. Stacey / play volleyball
2. Manuela / snowboard 
3. Leo / swim 
4. Alex / play pool 
5. Jesse and Ken / play soccer 
6. Dara / do martial arts 

E **Grammar Talk!** Can he swim? Student A page 101, Student B page 104.

I can... use *can* to talk about ability.   ☐ Very well   ☐ Well   ☐ Not very well

56

4 READING AND WRITING

A Read and listen to the article. Do you think you can do this sport? Why or why not?

CAN YOU PADDLEBOARD?

Paddleboarding is a very popular new water sport. Paddleboarders stand on boards and push the boards with long paddles. It looks difficult, but it is very easy. Can you stand up? Can you swim? Then you can paddleboard.

Paddleboarding is a wonderful way to spend time on the ocean or on a lake. It's a lot of fun, but it's also great exercise. You use your legs and the middle of your body for balance. You use your arms to paddle. It gives your whole body a workout.

You don't need a lot of equipment for paddleboarding. You just need a board, a paddle, water, and yourself!

B Read again. Write **T** (true) or **F** (false) next to the sentences. Correct the false sentences.
___ 1. Paddleboarding is an old sport.
___ 2. It's very difficult.
___ 3. It's great exercise.
___ 4. You can paddleboard on the ocean or on a lake.
___ 5. You need a lot of different things for paddleboarding.

C What sports can you do? What sports can't you do? Complete the chart.

I can	I can't
play tennis	

WRITING
Using *and* and *but*
Use *and* to connect two similar ideas. Use *but* to connect two opposite ideas.

ONLINE PRACTICE

D Write a paragraph about sports you can or can't do.

I can do some sports, but not others. For example, I can _____ , but I can't _____ . I can _____ and _____ , but I can't _____ .

I can... use *and* and *but* when I write. ☐ Very well ☐ Well ☐ Not very well

UNIT 9   57

5 VIEWING: Brush boarding

A Look at the photo. Write three questions about brush boarding.

1. _____?
2. _____?
3. _____?

B Watch the video. Does it answer any of your questions from Part A?

C Watch again. Circle the correct word in each sentence.

1. If you can surf or *snowboard / do yoga*, you can brush board.
2. You can brush board in any kind of *clothes / weather*.
3. You can brush board without *water / equipment* or snow.
4. Brush boarding isn't *fun / easy*.
5. Young children *can / can't* brush board.
6. To brush board, you need *good balance / a lot of money*.

> **VIEWING**
> **Asking questions**
> Ask questions about the video before you watch. This helps you focus as you watch.
>
> ONLINE PRACTICE

D Ask classmates the questions below. Find someone who answers *Yes*. Write the person's name in the chart.

Questions	Name
1. Do you have good balance?	
2. Can you surf?	
3. Can you snowboard?	
4. Can you swim?	
5. Do you want to brush board?	

I can... ask questions before I watch. ☐ Very well ☐ Well ☐ Not very well

6 PRESENTING

A Look at the photos and read the presentation. Check the photo that the presentation *does not* describe.

> **❝** Broom hockey is a really fun sport. You can play it outdoors on ice or pavement. You can also play it indoors, in a gym or other big space. You can play it any time of year, in any kind of weather. You don't need much equipment – just some brooms and a ball. It's very cheap, and it's easy to learn. So get some friends together and try broom hockey! **❞**

> **PRESENTING**
> **Supporting ideas with photos**
> Use photos to show how something looks or to describe something. Photos make your presentation interesting.
>
> ONLINE PRACTICE

B Read the presentation again. Answer the questions.
1. Where can you play broom hockey?
2. Can you play broom hockey in all the seasons – spring, summer, fall, winter?
3. What equipment do you need?
4. Is it easy to learn?
5. Is it expensive?

C Think of an unusual sport or look on the Internet for ideas. Take notes about the sport. Find photos of the sport.

Sport _____

- Where can you play it?
- In what season can you play?
- What equipment do you need?
- Is it easy to learn?
- Is it expensive?

TIP

Hold your photos so everyone in your audience can see them.

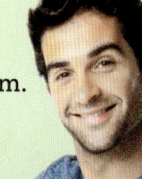

D Stand up. Use your notes from Part C to tell a group about the sport. Show your photos to the group as you speak.

PRESENT

> **I can...** use photos to support my ideas.   ☐ Very well   ☐ Well   ☐ Not very well

59

Self-Assessment

1 VOCABULARY

Circle the correct word or words to complete each sentence.

1. Let's eat dinner in the *bedroom* / *dining room* / *hall*.
2. Jack is in the *bathroom* / *kitchen* / *living room*. He's taking a shower.
3. The car is in the *bedroom* / *balcony* / *garage*.
4. Please put your clothes in the *yard* / *closet* / *stairs*.

I can... understand vocabulary about a house. (Unit 7)

5. Let's *go to the movies* / *eat out* / *play video games*. I want to see the new comedy.
6. Kim wants to *work out at the gym* / *watch TV* / *go shopping*. She wants to buy new shoes.
7. I usually *hang out with friends* / *eat out* / *work out at the gym* on Saturday nights. We cook dinner and talk.

I can... understand vocabulary about free time activities. (Unit 8)

8. I never *play volleyball* / *go snowboarding* / *do martial arts*. I don't like cold weather.
9. The weather is beautiful today. Let's *go swimming* / *play pool* / *do martial arts*.
10. Sarah has a nice bike. She *does yoga* / *plays volleyball* / *goes biking* every day.

I can... understand vocabulary about sports. (Unit 9)

2 GRAMMAR

1. This is a big apartment. *There is* / *There are* / *Are there* four bedrooms.
2. *Is there* / *Are there* / *There is* a big closet in the bedroom?
3. The bedrooms are *in* / *at* / *on* the second floor.

I can... use *there is/there are* and prepositions of place. (Unit 7)

4. When *do you work* / *you work* / *you do work* out at the gym?
5. How often *do Lisa goes* / *Lisa goes* / *does Lisa go* shopping?
6. Ken plays video games twice *week* / *a week* / *weeks*.
7. I exercise *in* / *at* / *on* the morning.

I can... ask and answer *Wh-* questions in the simple present. (Unit 8)

8. James *can speaks* / *can speak* / *can speaking* Korean.
9. I *can't swim* / *can't swimming* / *can't swims*.
10. *He can't* / *He can* / *Can he* play basketball?

I can... use *can* to talk about ability. (Unit 9)

60

Units 7-9

3 READING

A Read and listen to the information. Where does Carlos go to school?

Carlos Fuente

Basic Information

Birthday: May 14
Email address: carlosfuente@kmail.com
City: Los Angeles, CA
School: Kimball College

I'm a university student. I'm studying music. I play the piano and the guitar. I can also speak Spanish and Portuguese. In my free time, I like to hang out with my friends in my apartment. We never eat out. I cook dinner every night. The kitchen is my favorite room in my apartment.

I don't really like to play volleyball and baseball. I like to watch soccer on TV. I work out at the gym three times a week. There are a lot of bikes at my gym, but I don't like biking.

B Read each statement. Write **T** (true) or **F** (false). Correct the false statements.

____ 1. Carlos is a student.
____ 2. Carlos likes to eat out with his friends.
____ 3. Carlos can cook.
____ 4. Carlos never watches soccer on TV.
____ 5. Carlos works out at home.

C Read again. Answer the questions.

1. Can Carlos play the piano?
2. Who does Carlos hang out with in his free time?
3. How often does Carlos cook dinner?
4. Where does Carlos work out?
5. How often does Carlos work out?

D Answer the questions about you.

1. How often do you work out?
2. What languages can you speak?
3. What is your favorite room in your house?

10 Big events

Listening
Listening for time phrases

Speaking
Showing enthusiasm

Grammar
be going to; Yes/No questions

Reading
Taking notes

Viewing
Understanding data

Presenting
Standing up straight (2)

1 VOCABULARY AND LISTENING

A Listen and repeat.
CD 2-22

1. start school
2. get a job 
3. take guitar lessons 
4. graduate from high school 
5. move 
6. take a vacation 
7. go on a date 
8. celebrate a birthday 

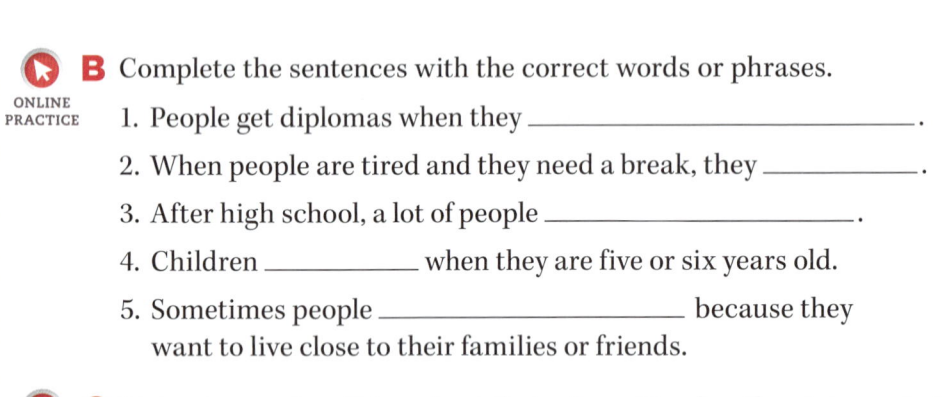

B Complete the sentences with the correct words or phrases.

1. People get diplomas when they _____.
2. When people are tired and they need a break, they _____.
3. After high school, a lot of people _____.
4. Children _____ when they are five or six years old.
5. Sometimes people _____ because they want to live close to their families or friends.

> **LISTENING**
> **Listening for time phrases**
> Time words and phrases like *tomorrow*, *next month*, and *next Friday* often come at the end of a sentence.
>
> ONLINE PRACTICE

C Listen to people talking about their plans. Number the pictures *1–4*.
CD 2-23

a.   b.    c.    d.

D Listen Again When is each event? Check the correct time.
CD 2-23

1. ☐ next weekend
   ☐ next month
   ☐ next week

2. ☐ next weekend
   ☐ next Wednesday
   ☐ next week

3. ☐ next weekend
   ☐ next month
   ☐ next week

4. ☐ next weekend
   ☐ next month
   ☐ next week

> **I can...** listen for time phrases about big events.   ☐ Very well   ☐ Well   ☐ Not very well

2 SPEAKING

A Fill in the blanks with words from the box.

| excited | friends | stay | summer |

1. Are you going to take a vacation this _____?
2. Are you going to go with your _____?
3. Are you going to _____ there long?
4. I'm so _____!

B Listen to the conversation. Then practice with a partner.

CD 2-24

> **SPEAKING**
> **Showing enthusiasm**
> Show enthusiasm when you're happy about something. Use expressions like *Fabulous, Wow,* and *Great.*
>
> ONLINE PRACTICE

Dan: Are you going to take a vacation soon?
Rita: Yes, I am. I'm going to go to Hawaii.
Dan: Fabulous! Are you going to go with your parents?
Rita: No, with my cousin.
Dan: Are you going to stay there long?
Rita: Yes. Three weeks.
Dan: Wow! Great!
Rita: Yeah, I'm really excited.

C Work in pairs. Practice the conversation below with your own information.

A: Are you going to take a vacation soon?
B: Yes, I am. I'm going to go to _____.
A: Fabulous! Are you going to go with your _____?
B: No, _____ is going to go with me.

D Pronunciation *going to* Listen and repeat. *Going to* is reduced to *gonna* in informal English.

CD 2-25

1. Are you **going to** take a vacation soon?
2. I'm **going to** go to London.
3. My sister is **going to** go with me.
4. I'm **going to** miss you.

I can... show enthusiasm.   ☐ Very well   ☐ Well   ☐ Not very well

UNIT 10   63

3 GRAMMAR

A Listen. Then listen again and repeat.

Grammar Reference page 91

be going to: affirmative and negative statements; Yes/No questions	
I'**m going to** go to Thailand.	I'**m not going to** go to Vietnam.
He'**s going to** move to China. She'**s going to** travel in the summer.	He **isn't going to** live in Mexico. She **isn't going to** travel in the winter.
We'**re going to** see our family. They'**re going to** start school.	We **aren't going to** see our friends. They **aren't going to** get a job.
Are you **going to** take a vacation next week? **Is** he **going to** play tennis? **Are** they **going to** graduate this summer?	Yes, I **am**. / No, I'**m not**. Yes, he **is**. / No, he **isn't**. Yes, they **are**. / No, they **aren't**.

B Match the questions with the answers.

___ 1. Is May going to graduate this year?
___ 2. Are you going to take a vacation soon?
___ 3. Is Luis going to visit his family this weekend?
___ 4. Are Ang and Carla going to move?
___ 5. Is the library going to close soon?

a. Yes, they are. They're going to rent a house.
b. No, it isn't.
c. Yes, she is. She's going to graduate in August.
d. No, I'm not.
e. Yes, he is. He's going to drive to their house.

C Work in pairs. Ask questions and give answers.

Example:
Eric / move
A: Is Eric going to move?
B: Yes, he is.

1. they / take a vacation
2. Alison / start school this year 
3. Marcus and Petra / go on a date this Friday 
4. Sylvia / graduate this year 
5. Paul / go home early 
6. Mia / take piano lessons 

D Grammar Talk! Is she going to move? Student A page 101, Student B page 104.

I can... use *be going to* to talk about the future.   ☐ Very well   ☐ Well   ☐ Not very well

64

4 READING AND WRITING

A Read and listen. What is the article about?

MATSON UNIVERSITY NEWS

Interview Question of the Week:
It's the end of the school year. What are you going to do this summer?

JOANIE CHANG
I'm going to take a vacation this summer. I'm going to spend two months in Europe. My two best friends are going to go with me. It's going to be fun.

CARLOS LOPEZ
My brother and I are going to live at our parents' house and get jobs. We're going to stay there for three months. We're not going to go on vacation. We're going to save money because we want to go on a really nice vacation next year.

PAM CRUISE
My roommates and I are going to stay here at the university for ten weeks. We're going to take some summer classes.

B Read again. Complete the chart with the correct information.

	Where?	What?	How long?	With who?
Joanie				
Carlos				
Pam				

**READING
Taking notes**
Taking notes as you read helps you focus on your reading. Write down only the important information.

ONLINE PRACTICE

C Imagine that it's the end of the school year. Make summer plans. Make notes in the chart.

Where?	What?	How long?	With who?

D Write about your summer plans. Use your notes from Part C.

This summer, I'm going to go to _____. I'm going to be there for _____. _____ is going to _____ with me.

I can... take notes as I read. ☐ Very well ☐ Well ☐ Not very well

5 VIEWING: Gap year

A Look at the photo and the map. What do you think the girl is going to do soon?

B Watch the video. Write the correct answers. More than one answer is possible.

1. A gap year is ___.
   a. a year off between high school and college
   b. the last year of high school
   c. the first year of college

2. A gap year often ___.
   a. helps students get good grades in college
   b. helps students get a job after college
   c. makes teachers angry

3. Before a gap year, it's a good idea to ___.
   a. buy furniture
   b. make a plan
   c. take a vacation

CULTURE TALK!

Many students in the U.K. and Australia take a gap year. Do many people in your country take a gap year?

C Watch again. Read the statements. Write **T** (true) or **F** (false).

___ 1. Antonia is going to graduate from high school next month.
___ 2. Antonia is going to go to college this year.
___ 3. Antonia is going to travel to Spain and Germany.
___ 4. Antonia is going to visit France next summer.
___ 5. 50% of students said their gap year helped their grades.
___ 6. 57% of students said their gap year helped them find a job after college.
___ 7. Trudy studied in Boston during her gap year.
___ 8. Trudy lived in Boston for one year.

VIEWING
Understanding data
Look carefully at graphics and pay attention to words like numbers and percentages. They help you understand data.

ONLINE PRACTICE

D What are some good things and bad things about taking a gap year? Make a list. Then talk about your ideas with a partner.

I can... understand data. ☐ Very well ☐ Well ☐ Not very well

6 PRESENTING

A Read the presentation. What three things is Daniel going to do during his gap year?

1. _____
2. _____
3. _____

PRESENTING
Standing up straight (2)
Remember to stand up straight when you give a presentation. Keep your head up and your shoulders back.

ONLINE PRACTICE

"My name's Daniel. I'm 17 years old. After high school, I'm going to take a gap year. First, I'm going to work in a restaurant for a few months to save money. Then I'm going to go backpacking around Southeast Asia. After that, I'm going to teach English to children in South Korea. It's going to be a great year. I can't wait!"

B Read the presentation to a partner. Remember to stand up straight.

C Imagine you are going to take a gap year. Make notes in the chart.

Where?	
What?	
How long?	

TIP

Before you give a presentation, practice in front of a mirror.

D Stand up. Use your notes from Part C. Tell a group about your gap year plans. Remember to stand up straight.

PRESENT

I can... stand up straight when I give a presentation. ☐ Very well ☐ Well ☐ Not very well

11 Plans

Listening
Listening for plans

Grammar
be going to; Wh-questions

Viewing
Using photos to make predictions

Speaking
Accepting an invitation

Writing
Writing a revision

Presenting
Looking up (2)

1 VOCABULARY AND LISTENING

A Listen and repeat.
CD 2-28

1. watch a DVD
2. visit a museum 
3. go away 
4. spend time with my family 
5. study for an exam 
6. see friends 
7. stay home and read 
8. work 

B Complete each sentence with a word or phrase from Part A.

1. I'm going to _____ tonight. I am tired and I want to relax.
2. I _____ from 9:00 a.m. to 5:00 p.m., then I go home.
3. This Saturday, I'm going to _____ and look at paintings.
4. There aren't any good shows on TV, so I'm going to _____. I like comedies.
5. I usually _____ on the weekend. I like to travel.

C Listen to people talking about weekend plans. What are their plans? Circle the correct answer.
CD 2-29

1. a. study for an exam   b. spend time with family
2. a. stay home   b. go out to dinner
3. a. watch sports on TV   b. watch a DVD
4. a. eat out   b. go shopping

> **LISTENING**
> **Listening for plans**
> Plans show what we decide to do in the future. The words after *going to* tell you about a speaker's plans.
>
> ONLINE PRACTICE

D Listen Again Write **T** (true) or **F** (false) next to the sentences. Correct the false sentences.
CD 2-29

___ 1. He's going to be with his family.   ___ 3. He's going to be alone.
___ 2. She's going to be with friends.   ___ 4. He's going to be with friends.

> **I can...** listen for weekend plans.   ☐ Very well   ☐ Well   ☐ Not very well

2 SPEAKING

A Match the questions and answers.

___ 1. What are you going to do this weekend?
___ 2. Is Brian going to go with you?
___ 3. Are you going to do anything special?
___ 4. Do you have plans for the weekend?

a. No, I'm going to go with my friend Jake.
b. Yes, I do. I'm going to get together with friends.
c. I'm going to visit my sister.
d. No. Nothing much.

B Listen to the conversation. Then practice with a partner.
CD 2-30

Karen: Do you have any special plans this weekend?
Scott: No. Not really. I'm going to stay home and read. How about you?
Karen: I have a lot of plans. I'm going to visit a museum on Saturday morning. Then I'm going to play tennis on Saturday afternoon.
Scott: Who are you going to play tennis with?
Karen: With my friend Linda. We always play tennis on Saturdays.
Scott: Cool.
Karen: I'm going to see a movie with friends on Sunday night. Do you want to come?
Scott: **Sure, I'd love to!**

SPEAKING
Accepting an invitation
Use an expressions like *Sure, I'd love to!* or *That sounds great!* to accept an invitation.

ONLINE PRACTICE

C Work in pairs. Practice the conversation below with your own information.

A: What plans do you have for the weekend?
B: Well, I'm going to _____ on Saturday, and I'm going to _____ on Sunday.
A: Great!
B: What about you? Do you have any plans?
A: I'm going to _____ on Saturday, and I'm going to _____ on Sunday. Do you want to come?
B: _____ .

CULTURE TALK!
In Brazil, young people often get together with friends on weekends to play soccer or volleyball. What do you do on weekends?

> **I can...** accept an invitation.   ☐ Very well   ☐ Well   ☐ Not very well

UNIT 11   69

3 GRAMMAR

A Listen. Then listen again and repeat.

Grammar Reference page 92

be going to; Wh- questions

What are you **going to do** on Saturday?	I**'m going to** visit my parents.
Where is he **going to be** on Sunday?	He**'s going to** be at home.
Who is she **going to be** with?	She**'s going to** be with her brother.
When are you **going to go** away?	We**'re going to go** away next weekend.
How long are they **going to stay**?	They**'re going to** stay for two hours.

B Read the answers and complete the questions. Then practice with a partner.

1. A: _____ are you going to go on Saturday?   B: I'm going to go to my friend's house.
2. A: _____ are you going to stay at the beach?   B: About four hours.
3. A: _____ are you going to do on Sunday?   B: I'm going to stay home and read.
4. A: _____ are you going to leave for school?   B: At 8:00 a.m.
5. A: _____ are you going to play soccer with?   B: My roommate.

C **Pronunciation** Reduction of *are* Listen and repeat. Notice that *are* sounds like *er* in these questions.

1. What **are** you going to do?
2. How long **are** you going to stay?
3. Where **are** you going to go?
4. Who **are** you going to go with?

D Work in pairs. Ask questions and give answers.

Example:
what / Eduardo / do?
A: What is Eduardo going to do this weekend?
B: He's going to visit a museum.

1. when / Vince / go away
2. where / Amy / go 
3. what / they / do 
4. who / Rita / visit 
5. where / they / study 
6. what / Tomas / do 

E **Grammar Talk!** Where is she going to go? Student A page 102, Student B page 105.

I can... ask and answer Wh- questions with *be going to*.   ☐ Very well   ☐ Well   ☐ Not very well

4 READING AND WRITING

A Read and listen to the article. Choose the correct title.

a. Weekend Plans in the City   b. What Are You Going to Do This Summer?   c. People at Work

It's going to be really hot this weekend!
What are people in the city going to do?

Pablo Valdez
My friends and I are going to play soccer on Saturday. On Sunday, I'm going to study for an exam. I have a history test next week.

Robert Lyle
I'm not going to do anything special. I'm going to stay home and work in the garden. I'm probably going to read and listen to music.

Lisa Ray
I'm going to go to my niece's graduation ceremony. She's going to graduate from high school on Saturday.

WRITING
Writing a revision
After you write something, check it carefully for correct punctuation and grammar. Then, write a revision.

ONLINE PRACTICE

B Read again. Answer the questions.

1. Who is going to take a test?
2. Who is going to go to a graduation?
3. Who is going to play soccer?
4. Who is going to stay home?

C Write questions using the cues below. Then interview a classmate and write your classmate's answers.

1. what / do / this Saturday _____?
   _____

2. who / be with _____?
   _____

3. what / do / this Sunday _____?
   _____

4. your own idea _____?
   _____

D Work with a partner. Read your partner's interview in Part C. Check your partner's sentences. Circle *Yes* or *No* below.

All sentences start with capital letters.	Yes	No
All questions end with question marks.	Yes	No
All statements end with periods.	Yes	No
My partner uses *be going to* correctly.	Yes	No

I can... write a revision.   ☐ Very well   ☐ Well   ☐ Not very well

UNIT 11   71

5 VIEWING: A weekend in Bali

A Look at the photo and the map, and make predictions. Answer the questions below.

1. What is the woman going to do?
2. What is she going to see?
3. Is she going to have fun?

B What does Mohini do in Bali? Check ✓ your answers.

- ☐ plays tennis
- ☐ goes scuba diving
- ☐ takes a boat ride
- ☐ sees a lot of fish
- ☐ goes shopping
- ☐ visits a museum

> **VIEWING**
> **Using photos to make predictions**
> Look at photos and make predictions before you watch. This helps you to understand a video.
>
> ONLINE PRACTICE

C Watch again. Complete the sentences. Use words from the box.

| water | fish | meters | boats | reef ✓ | divers |

1. Mohini is going to scuba dive at a tropical ___reef___.
2. Many dive _____ leave from Ginimanuk seaport.
3. Menjangan is a good place for expert or beginner _____.
4. The _____ is very clear.
5. They are going to dive down to about ten _____.
6. The _____ are beautiful and colorful.

D Work in a small group. Discuss the questions.

1. Do you know how to scuba dive? If not, do you want to try it?
2. Scuba diving is an exciting activity. What are some other exciting activities?
3. What exciting activities do you want to try? Are you going to try any of them this year?

I can... use photos to make predictions.   ☐ Very well   ☐ Well   ☐ Not very well

6 PRESENTING

A Read the invitation. Answer the questions below.

> PRESENTING
> **Looking up (2)**
> Look up at your audience when you are presenting. Quickly look down at your notes for important information.
>
> ONLINE PRACTICE

BBQ!

Let's get together and have some fun on the last weekend of summer. Please come to my house – 11 Pine Street – for a barbecue on Saturday, June 5, at around 4:00 p.m. There's going to be great food and music, and hopefully great weather, too. Hope you can come. Please RSVP by Thursday, June 3.

Jen

1. What is the event?
2. Why is Jen having the event?
3. When is it going to happen?
4. Where is it going to happen?

B Read the presentation to a partner and look up.

C You are going to invite your classmates to do something this weekend. Make notes below.

What? _____
Why?   _____
Where? _____
When? _____

TIP

Use a happy tone of voice – you are inviting your classmates to do something fun!

PRESENT D Stand up. Use your notes from Part C to invite a group of classmates to your event.

▶ **I can...** look up when I give a presentation. ☐ Very well ☐ Well ☐ Not very well

73

12 On vacation

Listening
Listening for tone (2)

Speaking
Responding to news

Grammar
Simple past

Reading
Using a mind map

Viewing
Understanding the order of events

Presenting
Making lists and speaking loudly

1 VOCABULARY AND LISTENING

A Listen and repeat.

1. went to Guam
2. arrived at the airport 
3. rented a car 
4. visited Tarzan Falls 
5. took a lot of photos 
6. ate delicious food 
7. had a good time 
8. came home 

B Complete each sentence with a verb from the box.

| arrived | ate | rented | visited | went |

1. I _____ to Seoul last year.
2. I _____ at a great restaurant in Rio.
3. We _____ at noon on Friday.
4. We _____ a car.
5. We _____ a lot of museums on vacation.

C Listen to people talking about vacations. Did they have a good time? Match the speakers to how they felt.

____ Speaker 1   a. had a bad time
____ Speaker 2   b. had an amazing time
____ Speaker 3   c. had an OK time
____ Speaker 4   d. had a great time

LISTENING
Listening for tone (2)
Tone can help you understand what a person is saying. Does the person sound happy? Sad? Excited?

ONLINE PRACTICE

D Listen Again. Number the activities from 1–4.

a.   b.    c.    d.

▶ **I can...** identify tone when listening about vacations.   ☐ Very well   ☐ Well   ☐ Not very well

74

2 SPEAKING

A Put the conversation in order. Number the sentences from *1–6*.

___ I went to Mexico.

___ Two weeks.

___ Did you have a good time there?

___ I had a fantastic time.

_1_ Hey, Alex. Where did you go on vacation?

___ Mexico? How long did you stay?

B Listen to the conversation. Then practice with a partner.
CD 2-36

SPEAKING
Responding to news
To respond to news, use expressions like *That sounds like fun!* and *How exciting!*

ONLINE PRACTICE

Kelly: Where did you go on vacation?

Sarah: I went to Washington, D.C., with one of my friends.

Kelly: That sounds like fun! How long did you stay?

Sarah: Just one week. How about you? Did you go away?

Kelly: No, I didn't. I stayed home.

Sarah: Really? What did you do?

Kelly: Nothing much. I slept late, I visited friends, I went out to eat.

Sarah: Sounds like you had fun and relaxed.

C Work in pairs. Practice the conversation below with your own information.

A: Where did you go on vacation?

B: I went to _____.

A: That sounds like fun! How long did you stay?

B: _____ days. How about you? Where did you go?

A: I went to _____.

B: How exciting!

D Pronunciation Reduction of *did you* Listen and repeat. Notice the reduction of *did you*.
CD 2-37

1. **Did you** go away?
2. Where **did you** go?
3. What **did you** do?
4. What **did you** see?

I can... respond to news. ☐ Very well ☐ Well ☐ Not very well

UNIT 12 75

3 GRAMMAR

A Listen. Then listen again and repeat.

Grammar Reference page 93

Simple past

Yes/No questions

Did you **go** to Vietnam?	No, I **didn't**. I **didn't go** to Vietnam.
Did she **enjoy** her vacation?	Yes, she **did**.
Did they **have** any problems?	No, they **didn't**.

Wh- questions

Where **did** you **go**?	I **went** to Hong Kong.
What **did** she **do**?	She **went** to a karaoke club.
When **did** they **come** home?	They **came** home last Sunday.

NOTE: Some verbs have irregular past tense forms: go – went, come – came, see – saw

B Complete the conversations. Use the simple past tense forms of the verbs in parentheses. Then practice the conversations with a partner.

1. A: Where _____ you _____ (go) last month?   B: I _____ (go) to Hawaii.
2. A: When _____ you _____ (arrive)?   B: I _____ (arrive) at 2:30.
3. A: What _____ you _____ (visit)?   B: We _____ (visit) museums.
4. A: _____ you _____ (enjoy) your trip?   B: I _____ (enjoy) it a lot.

C Work in pairs. Ask questions and give answers.

Example: what / Mia / do
A: What did Mia do?
B: She visited her grandmother.

1. where / Luis / go
2. who / Amy / go with 
3. what / Tomas / visit 
4. Sarah / have / any problems 
5. when / Sean and Pedro / come home 
6. Kimberly and Lynn / have a good time 

D Grammar Talk! What did he do last Monday? Student A page 102, Student B page 105.

I can... ask and answer *Wh-* questions in the simple past.   ☐ Very well   ☐ Well   ☐ Not very well

4 READING AND WRITING

A Read and listen. Where did Mina go?

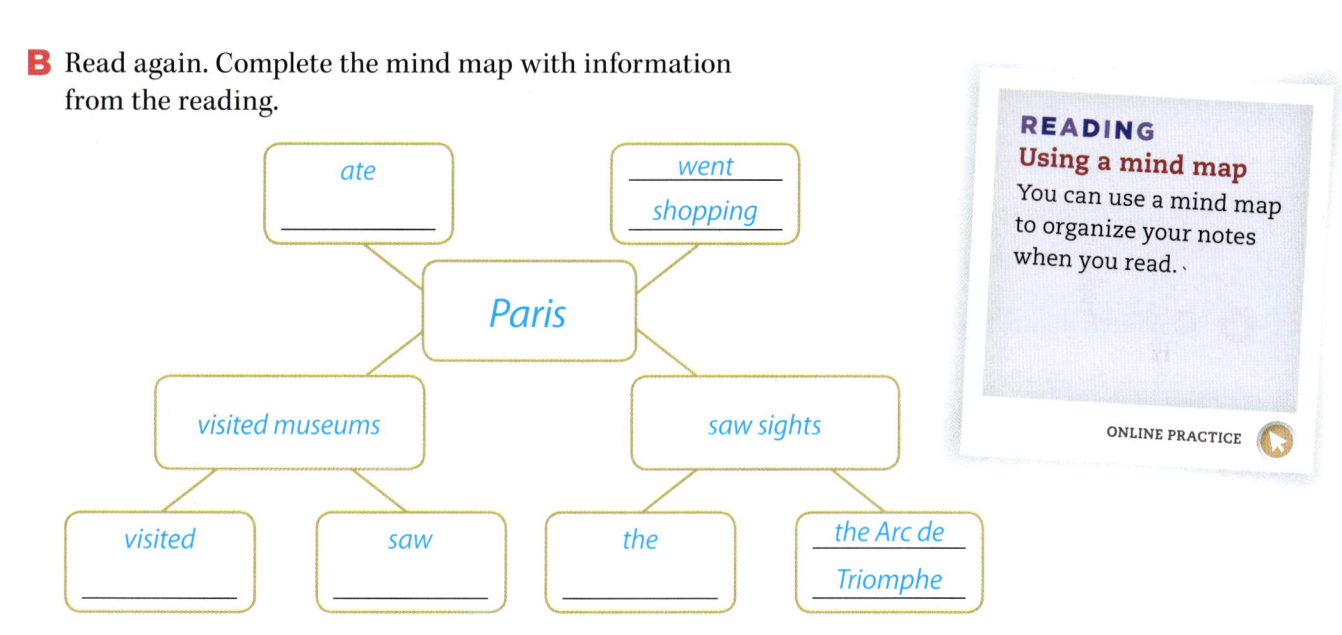

Mina King

I just came home from a great vacation. I went to Paris, France, with my friend Serena. We had a wonderful time. We visited a lot of museums. My favorite was the Louvre. We saw the Mona Lisa there. We walked around a lot, too. Paris is a beautiful city, and there is a lot to see. We saw a lot of sights, like the Eiffel Tower and the Arc de Triomphe. We also went shopping and ate a lot of delicious food. We stayed for a week. Next time, I'm going to stay for two weeks.

Profile
Photos (51)
Notes
Friends

LIKE COMMENT SHARE 2 HOURS AGO

Sandra May: I love Paris, too! It's my favorite city.

Kenneth Park: I'm going to go to Paris next summer!

B Read again. Complete the mind map with information from the reading.

- ate _____
- went shopping
- Paris
  - visited museums
    - visited _____
    - saw _____
  - saw sights
    - the _____
    - the Arc de Triomphe

READING
Using a mind map
You can use a mind map to organize your notes when you read.

ONLINE PRACTICE

C Make a mind map of a recent vacation. Put the location in the middle circle. Put things that you did in the outer circles.

D Use your mind map to write about a recent vacation.

I went to _____ for vacation in _____. _____ came with me.
We _____.
We _____, too.
We also _____. I had a _____ time.

I can... use a mind map to organize my notes. ☐ Very well ☐ Well ☐ Not very well

UNIT 12   77

5 VIEWING: Tourist or local?

A What do you know about Sydney? Talk to a partner. Then circle the correct words below.

1. A *local / tourist* lives in a place.   2. A *local / tourist* is on vacation in a place.

B Watch the video. What did Carmen do in Sydney? Number the events in order from *1–5*.

___ a. She went to a soccer game.
___ b. She talked to a hairdresser.
___ c. She went to the beach.
___ d. She took a bus.
___ e. She ate a meat pie.

VIEWING
Understanding the order of events
Pay attention to the order of events. To remember the order, take notes.

ONLINE PRACTICE

C Watch again. Read the statements. Write **T** (true) or **F** (false).

___ 1. Sydney has a lot of tourists.
___ 2. Carmen liked the meat pie.
___ 3. A lot of locals go to the beach near Tamarama.
___ 4. Carmen walked to the beach.
___ 5. Carmen went to the Sydney Olympic Park.
___ 6. The people at the soccer game were not nice.

CULTURE TALK!

People call locals in Sydney "Sydneysiders." What do people call locals in your city?

D Where do locals go in your city? How about tourists? Complete the chart. Then talk about your ideas with a partner.

	Locals	Tourists
Restaurants		
Outdoor places		
Other places		

> **I can...** understand the order of events.   ☐ Very well   ☐ Well   ☐ Not very well

6 PRESENTING

A Read the presentation. The presenter talks about four places in Portland, Maine. List them.

1. _____
2. _____
3. _____
4. _____

> **PRESENTING**
> **Making lists and speaking loudly**
> Make a list to organize your ideas. Add one comment for each point. When you present, speak loudly.
>
> ONLINE PRACTICE

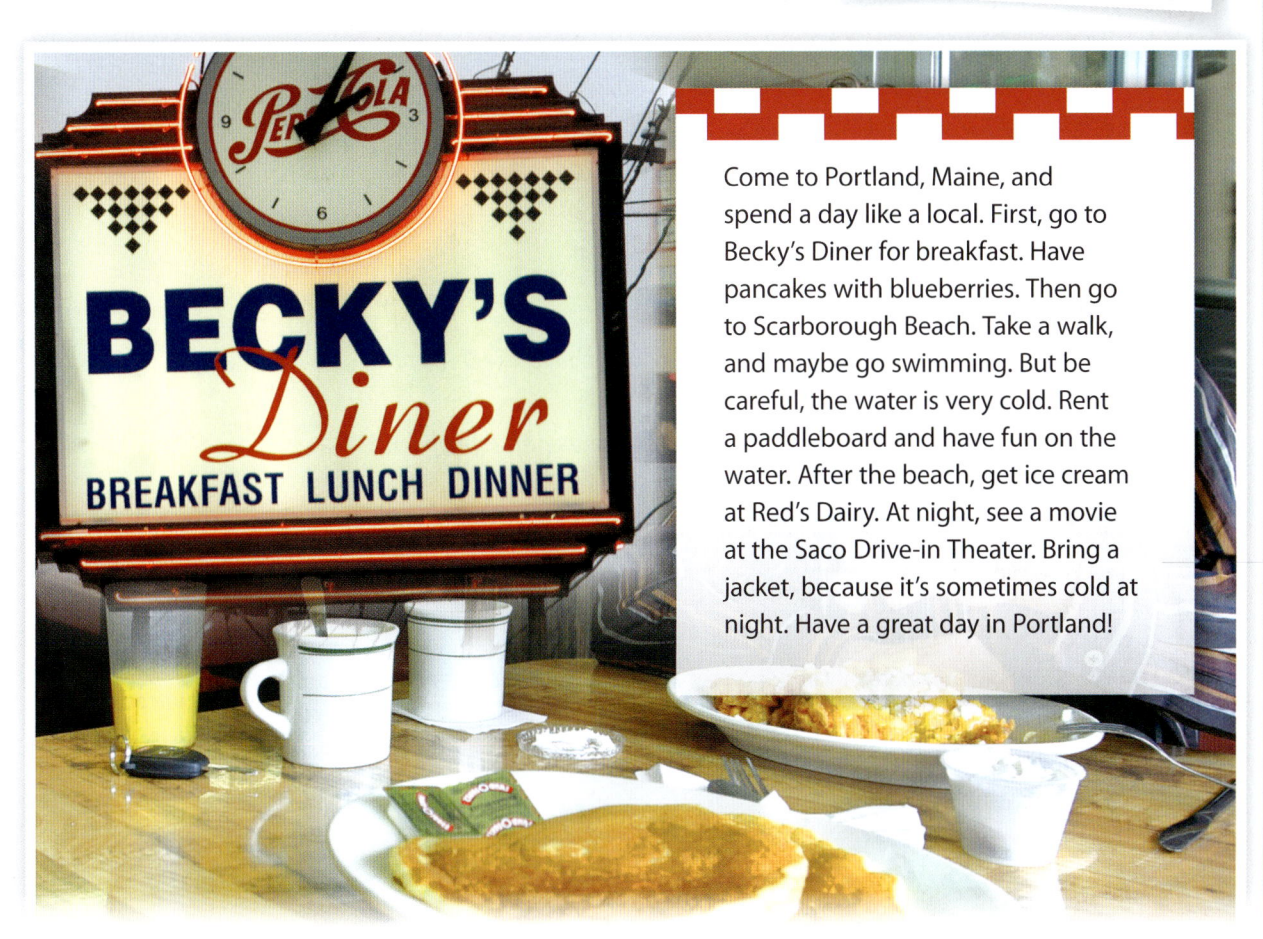

Come to Portland, Maine, and spend a day like a local. First, go to Becky's Diner for breakfast. Have pancakes with blueberries. Then go to Scarborough Beach. Take a walk, and maybe go swimming. But be careful, the water is very cold. Rent a paddleboard and have fun on the water. After the beach, get ice cream at Red's Dairy. At night, see a movie at the Saco Drive-in Theater. Bring a jacket, because it's sometimes cold at night. Have a great day in Portland!

B Read the presentation to a partner. Remember to speak loudly.

C A tourist wants to see your city like a local. Make a list of places to go.

1. _____
2. _____
3. _____
4. _____

D Stand up. Use your notes from Part C. Tell a group how to see your city like a local. Remember to speak loudly.

PRESENT

TIP
Smile when you are giving a presentation.

I can... make lists and speak loudly in presentations. ☐ Very well ☐ Well ☐ Not very well

Self-Assessment

1 VOCABULARY

Circle the correct word or words to complete each sentence.

1. My friends are going to take me out to dinner tomorrow to *go on a date* / *celebrate my birthday* / *get a job*. I'm going to be 21 years old.
2. Margo *wants to move* / *go on a date* / *start school*. She doesn't like her apartment.
3. Ken *takes guitar lessons* / *takes a vacation* / *graduates from high school* every summer. He usually goes to Mexico.

I can... understand vocabulary about big events. (Unit 10)

4. I like to *spend time with my family* / *go away* / *see friends*. I have dinner with my parents every weekend.
5. David and I are *studying for an exam* / *watching a DVD* / *working*. We have a big test next week.
6. Jackie is sick today. She's going to *visit a museum* / *see friends* / *stay home*.
7. We *move* / *go away* / *get a job* once a month. This weekend, we're going to go to the beach.

I can... understand vocabulary about weekend plans. (Unit 11)

8. Lisa *visited* / *arrived at* / *rented* the airport at 10:00 a.m.
9. We *took a lot of photos* / *came home* / *rented a car* on our trip. Do you want to see them?
10. I *rented a car* / *ate delicious food* / *arrived* in New York. There are a lot of great restaurants there.

I can... understand vocabulary about vacation. (Unit 12)

2 GRAMMAR

1. Karen and Joe *is going to* / *going to* / *are going to* graduate from high school next year.
2. I *isn't going to* / *'m not going to* / *aren't going to* take a vacation this summer.
3. *Is he going to* / *He's going to* / *He going to* go out tonight?

I can... use *be going to* to talk about the future. (Unit 10)

4. Where *are you* / *is you* / *you are* going to go this weekend?
5. How long *are Paul* / *Paul is* / *is Paul* going to stay with you?
6. *Where* / *When* / *Who* is Laura going to go with?

I can... ask and answer *Wh-* questions with *be going to*. (Unit 11)

7. We *going* / *go* / *went* to Chile last year.
8. Did you *enjoy* / *enjoyed* / *enjoys* your vacation last summer?
9. Carolyn *didn't visited* / *don't visited* / *didn't visit* her brother last weekend.
10. What *did Kim do* / *do Kim do* / *does Kim do* last night?

I can... ask and answer *Wh-* questions in the simple past. (Unit 12)

80

Units 10-12

3 READING

A Read and listen to the information. What is the writer's name?

To: Jodi Kim
From: Alison Martinez
Subject: News

Hi Jodi,

How are you? Everything is great here! We took a vacation in June. We went to beautiful Hawaii. We had a great time.

My husband Tom got a new job last week. He really likes it. He works with his friend Eduardo now. Eduardo helped Tom get the job.

Sarah's going to be 13 years old on Monday. We're going to celebrate her birthday this weekend. She wants to go out to dinner at her favorite restaurant. Her friend Gina is going to come with us.

Did you take a vacation this summer? Are you and your children going to visit us soon?

All the best,

Alison

B Read the statements. Write **T** (true) or **F** (false). Correct the false statements.

___ 1. Alison and her family are going to take a vacation in June.

___ 2. Eduardo is Alison's husband.

___ 3. Sarah turned 13 last Monday.

___ 4. Alison and her family are going to go out to dinner this weekend.

___ 5. Jodi doesn't have any children.

C Answer the questions.

1. Where did Alison and her family go for vacation?
2. When did Tom start his new job?
3. How old is Sarah going to be on Monday?
4. Who helped Tom get his job?
5. Who is going to go to dinner with Alison and her family?

D Imagine you are emailing an old friend. Tell your friend three things about your life and what you're doing now.

1. _____
2. _____
3. _____

SELF-ASSESSMENT | UNITS 10-12   81

GRAMMAR REFERENCE

Unit 1

To *be*; subject pronouns; possessive adjectives

We often use contractions with *be* in speaking.

- *I'm a student.*
- *Matt's a student.*
- *They're students.*

We don't usually use contractions with plural nouns and *are*.

- *Matt and Kendra are students.* **NOT** ~~*Matt and Kendra're students.*~~

We always use a noun after a possessive adjective.

- *This is my book.* **NOT** ~~*This book is my.*~~

Affirmative statements			Negative statements		
I	am / 'm	at home.	I	am not / 'm not	at work.
He		a student.	He		a teacher.
She	is / 's	at work.	She	is not / isn't	at school.
It		a car.	It		a truck.
You		nice.	You		mean.
We	are / 're	late.	We	are not / aren't	early.
They		happy.	They		sad.

Every subject pronoun has a possessive adjective.

Subject pronouns	Possessive adjectives
I	**My** name is Jane.
You	**Your** apartment is big.
He	**His** name is Kyle.
She	**Her** last name is Owens.
It	**Its** name is Snowball.
We	**Our** bus isn't here.
They	**Their** class is fun.

Grammar Practice!

1 Circle the correct word to complete each sentence.

1. This is my friend. (*His*) / *He* name is Matt.
2. This is my roommate. *Her* / *She* is a student.
3. Jackie is my neighbor. *Her* / *She* apartment number is 5B.
4. Jonas and Carl live downtown. *They* / *Their* address is 84 First Street.
5. Ken and I are from Japan. *We* / *Our* last name is Sato.

2 Complete each sentence with the correct form of *be*. Use contractions.

1. Jenna __'s__ a teacher.
2. We _____ students.
3. I _____ a nurse.
4. They _____ at work.
5. You _____ nice.

Unit 2

Yes/No questions and short answers with *be*

We often contract negative short answers.
- No, I**'m not**.
- No, he **isn't**.
- No, they **aren't**.

We only use full forms in affirmative short answers.
- Yes, I **am**.   NOT   ~~Yes, I'm.~~
- Yes, he **is**.   NOT   ~~Yes, he's.~~
- Yes, they **are**.   NOT   ~~Yes, they're.~~

Yes/No questions			Short answers	
Am	I	late?	Yes, I **am**.	No, I**'m not**.
Is	he / she / it	at home?	Yes, he **is**. / Yes, she **is**. / Yes, it **is**.	No, he **isn't**. / No, she **isn't**. / No, it **isn't**.
Are	you / we / they	neighbors?	Yes, we **are**. / Yes, you **are**. / Yes, they **are**.	No, we **aren't**. / No, you **aren't**. / No, they **aren't**.

Grammar Practice!

1 Put the words in the correct order to make questions.
1. is / at work / Michael — *Is Michael at work* ?
2. British / Andrea / are / John and _____ ?
3. late / I / am _____ ?
4. your / is / brother / here _____ ?
5. we / are / neighbors _____ ?
6. Kim / is / at home _____ ?
7. are / late / we _____ ?
8. is / ready / Luis _____ ?
9. Japanese / Tom / is _____ ?
10. Sally / from Brazil / is _____ ?

2 Complete each question with the correct form of *be*. Then match each question with an answer.

_d_ 1. ____*Are*____ you Japanese?   a. No, he isn't.
___ 2. _____ Roberto at work?   b. Yes, they are.
___ 3. _____ we late?   c. Yes, she is.
___ 4. _____ Carmelita a student?   d. Yes, I am.
___ 5. _____ they your friends?   e. No, you aren't.

GRAMMAR REFERENCE 83

Unit 3

Wh- questions with be

In *wh-* questions with *be*, look at the noun or pronoun to choose the correct form of *be*.

- Who's **he**?
- Who **are they**?
- What's his **name**?
- What **are** their **names**?

Who and *What* can be the subject of a question. In these questions, we use the singular form of *be*.

- What's wrong?
- Who's in the classroom?

Question words				
Use *what* … for things	Use *who* … for people	Use *where* … for places	Use *how* … for ways	Use *how old* … for age

Wh- questions			Answers
What	is	your name?	My name **is Derrick**.
Where	are	Jackie and Sarah?	They're **at school**.
Who	is	that?	That's my friend **Carrie**.
How	are	you?	I'm **fine**.
How old	is	your son?	He's **three years old**.

Grammar Practice!

1 Complete each question with the correct form of *be*.

1. What ___*are*___ their phone numbers?
2. Who _____ on the phone?
3. Where _____ you from?
4. How old _____ your brothers?
5. How _____ your mother?

2 Read the answers. Then write questions to complete the conversations.

1. A: _____ you?
   B: I'm fine.
2. A: _____ Tomas?
   B: He's 21 years old.
3. A: _____ Carl from?
   B: He's from Australia.
4. A: _____ your email address?
   B: It's gina33@yakadoo.com.
5. A: _____ that?
   B: That's my sister Lisa.

Unit 4

Have: affirmative and negative statements; Yes/No questions

We use the base form of *have* in negative statements and questions.

- *She doesn't **have** black hair.* **NOT** ~~*She doesn't **has** black hair.*~~

Affirmative statements			Negative statements		
I / You / We / They	have	blue eyes. brown hair.	I / You / We / They	don't have	brown eyes. blond hair.
He / She / It	has		He / She / It	doesn't have	

Yes/No questions			Short answers	
Do	I / you / we / they	have brown eyes?	Yes, you **do**. Yes, we **do**. Yes, you **do**. Yes, they **do**.	No, you **don't**. No, we **don't**. No, you **don't**. No, they **don't**.
Does	he / she / it		Yes, he **does**. Yes, she **does**. Yes, it **does**.	No, he **doesn't**. No, she **doesn't**. No, it **doesn't**.

Grammar Practice!

1 Complete each sentence with the correct affirmative or negative form of *have*.

1. Margaret's eyes are blue. Margaret ____*has*____ blue eyes.
2. Alan and Michael's hair is brown. Alan and James _____ black hair.
3. My eyes are green. I _____ green eyes.
4. Your hair is blond. You _____ brown hair.
5. Our eyes are brown. We _____ blue eyes.

2 Write questions to complete the conversations. Use the words in parentheses.

1. A: ____*Does she have green eyes*____? (green eyes)
   B: No, she doesn't.
2. A: _____? (brown hair)
   B: Yes, they do.
3. A: _____? (blond hair)
   B: Yes, he does.
4. A: _____? (blue eyes)
   B: No, she doesn't.
5. A: _____? (black hair)
   B: Yes, they do.

GRAMMAR REFERENCE 85

Unit 5

Simple present: affirmative and negative statements; Yes/No questions

We use the base form of a verb in negative statements and questions.

- *She doesn't **like** chicken.*   **NOT**   ~~*She doesn't **likes** chicken.*~~

Affirmative statements			Negative statements		
I			I		
You	**like**	pizza.	You	**don't like**	fish.
We		coffee.	We		tea.
They		carrots.	They		French fries.
He			He		
She	**likes**		She	**doesn't like**	
It			It		

Yes/No questions			Short answers	
	I		Yes, you **do**.	No, you **don't**.
Do	you		Yes, I **do**.	No, I **don't**.
	we	**like** tea?	Yes, you **do**.	No, you **don't**.
	they	**eat** lunch every day?	Yes, they **do**.	No, they **don't**.
	he	**work** on Mondays?	Yes, he **does**.	No, he **doesn't**.
Does	she		Yes, she **does**.	No, she **doesn't**.
	it		Yes, it **does**.	No, it **doesn't**.

Grammar Practice!

1 Look at the chart. Complete each sentence with the correct affirmative (✓) or negative form (✗) of *like*.

	chicken	fish	steak	spaghetti
Kim	✓	✗	✓	✗
Eric	✗	✓	✓	✗

1. Kim ____*doesn't like*____ fish.
2. Eric _____ fish.
3. Kim _____ chicken.
4. Kim and Eric _____ steak.
5. Kim and Eric _____ spaghetti.

2 Write questions with the words provided. Then answer the questions with short answers.

1. A: Luis / eat / steak _____ ?   B: No, he _____ .
2. A: you / like / coffee _____ ?   B: Yes, I _____ .
3. A: the restaurant / have / pizza _____ ?   B: No, it _____ .
4. A: I / work / every day _____ ?   B: No, you _____ .
5. A: Sue and May / like / fish _____ ?   B: Yes, they _____ .

86

Unit 6

Present continuous: affirmative and negative statements; Yes/No questions

We use the present continuous to talk about what is happening right now.

Affirmative statements			Negative statements		
I	'm		I	'm not	
He She It	's	working. eating. sleeping.	He She It	isn't	studying. driving. walking.
You We They	're		You We They	aren't	

Yes/No questions			Short answers	
Am	I		Yes, you **are**.	No, you **aren't**.
Is	he she it	working? eating? sleeping?	Yes, he **is**. Yes, she **is**. Yes, it **is**.	No, he **isn't**. No, she **isn't**. No, it **isn't**.
Are	you we they		Yes, I **am**. Yes, you **are**. Yes, they **are**.	No, I'm **not**. No, you **aren't**. No, they **aren't**.

Grammar Practice!

1 Complete each sentence with the correct affirmative or negative forms of the verbs in bold.

1. Mina **cooks** dinner at 6:00. It is 6:00 now. Mina _____ dinner now.
2. Alex **works** on Mondays and Tuesdays. Today is Friday. Alex _____ today.
3. We **talk** on the phone at 5:00. It is 3:30 now. We _____ on the phone now.
4. You **take** a shower at 8:00. It's 8:00 now. You _____ a shower now.
5. I **study** in the evenings. It's morning right now. I _____ now.

2 Write questions with the words provided. Then answer the questions with short answers.

1. A: Joanne / work _____?
   B: Yes, _____.
2. A: Mike / cook / dinner _____?
   B: Yes, _____.
3. A: you / shop _____?
   B: No, _____. I'm working.
4. A: Nina and Daniel / study _____?
   B: Yes, _____.
5. A: Eddie and Mark / text _____?
   B: No, _____. They're studying.

GRAMMAR REFERENCE 87

Unit 7

There is/There are; *Yes/No* questions; prepositions of place

We use *there is* with singular nouns and *there are* with plural nouns. We can use *any* with plural nouns in negative statements and questions.

Statements with singular nouns		Statements with plural nouns	
There's	**a bedroom** on the first floor. **a closet** in the bathroom.	There are	**three bedrooms**. **some clothes** in the closet.
There isn't	**a garage**. **a bathroom** on the first floor.	There aren't	**any closets** in the bathroom. **any apartments** for rent.

We can use *there are no* instead of *there aren't any*.
- There are no closets in the bathroom. = There aren't any closets in the bathroom.

Yes/No questions		Short answers
Is there	a dining room? a closet in the bedroom?	Yes, there **is**. No, there **isn't**.
Are there	two bathrooms? any two-bedroom apartments?	Yes, there **are**. No, there **aren't**.

In		On	
the bedroom the hall	the garage the yard	the first floor the top floor	the balcony the stairs

Grammar Practice!

1 Use the cues to write sentences with *there is/there are* and *in* or *on*.

1. two closets / the bedroom ____*There are two closets in the bedroom*____.
2. one bedroom / the second floor _____.
3. a car / the garage _____.
4. three trees / the yard _____.
5. a bathroom / the second floor _____.

2 Complete the questions with *Is there/Are there any* and the correct prepositions. Complete the answers with *there is*, *there isn't*, *there are*, or *there aren't*.

1. A: _____ chairs _____ the balcony?   B: No, _____.
2. A: _____ a living room _____ the apartment?   B: Yes, _____.
3. A: _____ cars _____ the garage?   B: Yes, _____.
4. A: _____ a bathroom _____ the top floor?   B: No, _____.
5. A: _____ a tree _____ the yard?   B: Yes, _____.

Unit 8

Simple present: *Wh-* questions

We use time expressions to answer questions with *when*. We use adverbs and expressions of frequency to answer questions with *how often*.

- I have lunch at home **every day**.
- I **usually** have lunch at home.

We usually put time expressions and phrases like *once a week* at the end of a sentence.

- I work **on Mondays**.   NOT   ~~I on Mondays work.~~

We put *never* before a verb.

- I **never** play video games.   NOT   ~~I play video games never.~~

Wh- questions	Answers
What do you **do?**	I'm a teacher.
Where does he **live?**	He lives in Dallas.
Who do they **live with?**	With their mother.
When does he **work?**	On Mondays and Fridays.
How often does she **play soccer?**	Three times a week.

Time expressions	Adverbs of frequency
every day	always
on Mondays and Fridays	usually
in the mornings	sometimes
in the afternoons	rarely
in the evenings	never

Grammar Practice!

1 Complete each question with *do* or *does*. Then match each question with the correct answer.

   _d_ 1. Where _____ your sister live?   a. She's a nurse.
   ___ 2. Who _____ you play tennis with?   b. Never.
   ___ 3. How often _____ he work out?   c. In the evenings.
   ___ 4. What _____ Jill do?   d. In New York.
   ___ 5. When _____ they study?   e. With Tanya.

2 Write questions. Use the words provided.

   1. where / Kate / work out _____?
   2. what / your parents / do _____?
   3. when / you / leave for work _____?
   4. who / she / study with _____?
   5. how often / Mark / call you _____?

GRAMMAR REFERENCE   89

Unit 9

Using *can* for ability

Can is a modal verb. Modal verbs have the same form for all subjects. We use a modal verb and the base form of the verb.

Affirmative statements			Negative statements		
I He She It You We They	**can**	**play** soccer. **swim**. **speak** Spanish.	I He She It You We They	**can't**	**do** yoga. **play** the piano well. **drive** a truck.

Yes/No questions			Short answers	
Can	I he she it you we they	**do** it? **sing**? **swim**? **fly**? **play** volleyball? **do** martial arts? **drive**?	Yes, you **can**. Yes, he **can**. Yes, she **can**. Yes, it **can**. Yes, I **can**. Yes, you **can**. Yes, they **can**.	No, you **can't**. No, he **can't**. No, she **can't**. No, it **can't**. No, I **can't**. No, you **can't**. No, they **can't**.

Grammar Practice!

1 Complete each sentence with *can* (✓) or *can't* (✗). Use the information in chart below.

	swim	play soccer	do yoga	drive
Lisa	✓	✗	✓	✓
Paul	✗	✓	✓	✗

1. Paul _____ play soccer.
2. Lisa _____ swim.
3. Paul _____ swim.
4. Lisa _____ play soccer.
5. Lisa _____ drive.
6. Paul and Lisa _____ do yoga.

2 Write questions with the words provided. Then write answers using information from the chart in Part 1.

1. A: Paul / drive _____? B: _____.
2. A: Lisa and Paul / do yoga _____? B: _____.
3. A: Lisa / drive _____? B: _____.
4. A: Paul / swim _____? B: _____.
5. A: Lisa / play soccer _____? B: _____.

Unit 10

be going to: affirmative and negative statements; Yes/No questions

We can use *be going to* for future plans. We use the base form of a verb after *be going to*.

Affirmative statements				Negative statements			
I	'm			I	'm not		
He				He			
She	's		move.	She	isn't		live with my parents.
It		going to	take a vacation.	It		going to	graduate.
You			study tonight.	You			go out.
We	're			We	aren't		
They				They			

Yes/No questions				Short answers	
Am	I			Yes, you **are**.	No, you **aren't**.
	he			Yes, he **is**.	No, he **isn't**.
Is	she		arrive soon?	Yes, she **is**.	No, she **isn't**.
	it	going to	work today?	Yes, it **is**.	No, it **isn't**.
	you		stay home?	Yes, I **am**.	No, I'm **not**.
Are	we			Yes, you **are**.	No, you **aren't**.
	they			Yes, they **are**.	No, they **aren't**.

Grammar Practice!

1 Complete each sentence with the correct form of *be going to* and the verb in parentheses.

1. Jesse _____ piano lessons. (take)
2. We _____ this year. (not / move)
3. I _____ a job this summer. (get)
4. _____ Erin _____ in June? (graduate)
5. _____ you _____ your birthday? (celebrate)

2 Write questions with the correct form of *be going to* and the words provided. Then answer the questions.

1. A: you / travel / this year _____?
   B: Yes, we _____ .
2. A: Sam / see his friends _____?
   B: No, he _____ .
3. A: I / be late _____?
   B: No, you _____ .
4. A: they / go on a date together _____?
   B: Yes, they _____ .
5. A: Kelly / start school / this fall _____?
   B: Yes, she _____ .

GRAMMAR REFERENCE 91

Unit 11

be going to: Wh- questions

We can use *be going to* with *Wh-* words to ask questions about future plans.
We often use *with* in questions with *who*.

Wh- questions					Answers
Where	am	I		go?	You're going to go to L.A.
What		he		eat for dinner?	He's going to have pizza.
Who	is	she		go with?	She's going to go with Julie.
When		it	going to	start?	At 8:00.
Why		you		move?	I don't like my apartment.
How long	are	we		wait?	We're going to wait for an hour.
How often		they		exercise?	Three times a week.

Grammar Practice!

1 Complete the questions with the correct forms of *be*. Then match each question with the correct answer.

___ 1. What _____ you going to do tonight? a. Because she's sick.
___ 2. Why _____ Ann going to stay home? b. We're going to stay with my aunt.
___ 3. How long _____ Jay and Franco going to study? c. Once a month.
___ 4. Where _____ Mina going to go to college? d. I'm going to watch a movie.
___ 5. Who _____ I going to ride with? e. For about two hours.
___ 6. How often _____ you going to visit your parents? f. You're going to ride with me.
___ 7. What _____ Kim going to do this weekend? g. She's going to study.
___ 8. Where _____ we going to stay? h. She's going to go to the University of Washington.

2 Write questions with the correct form of *be going to* and the words provided.

1. when / you / graduate from high school
   _____?

2. what / Stephen / cook for dinner
   _____?

3. where / Luke / stay
   _____?

4. how long / they / be here
   _____?

5. why / you / stay home
   _____?

6. how often / he / take guitar lessons
   _____?

Unit 12

Simple past

The past tense form is the same for most verbs. Regular verbs end in –d or –ed. Some verbs are irregular:

go → went   come → came   see → saw

We use *didn't* + the base form of a verb to make negative statements.

Affirmative statements		Negative statements		
I He She You We They	**went** to Hawaii. **came** home on Monday. **called** Shari.	I He She You We They	**didn't**	**go** to Hawaii. **come** home on Monday. **call** Shari.

Yes/No questions			Short answers			
Did	I he she you we they	**say** something? **go**? **eat** dinner?	Yes, you Yes, he Yes, she Yes, we Yes, you Yes, they	**did**.	No, you No, he No, she No, we No, you No, they	**didn't**.

To form a *Wh-* question in the simple past tense, use a *Wh-* word + *did* + subject + base form of the verb.

Wh- questions	Answers
Where did you **go**?	I **went** to New York.
What did you **do**?	We **visited** some museums.
How long did you **stay**?	We **stayed** for five days.

Grammar Practice!

1 Write statements in the simple past with the words in parentheses.

1. We _____ dinner at 7:00. (eat)
2. I _____ to work today. (not / go)
3. Gina _____ last night. (call)
4. Al _____ his family last year. (not / visit)
5. You _____ a great job! (do)

2 Write questions about the underlined words with the missing *Wh-* words and simple past verbs.

1. A: *Where did you go?* ?   B: I went to <u>a movie</u>.
2. A: _____ ?   B: She came <u>with James</u>.
3. A: _____ ?   B: They stayed <u>for a week</u>.
4. A: _____ ?   B: Jack went to <u>Alan's house</u>.
5. A: _____ ?   B: I called you <u>at 9:00</u>.

GRAMMAR REFERENCE   93

Grammar Talk!

1 What's his first name?
STUDENT A

Ask and answer questions with Student B to complete Christopher's class information form.

A: What's the teacher's name?
B: Ruby Kelly.

English 2A Class Information Form

Teacher's name: _____Ruby Kelly_____

Student's Information

First name: _____
Last name: Tang
Nickname: _____
Email address: cjtang@gotmail.com

Phone number: 555-_____
Address: 42 Lake Street, Apt. 14
Lakewood, NV, 89500

2 Where's he from?
STUDENT A

Ask and answer questions with Student B to complete the class list.

A: Where's Anita Perez from?
B: She's from Serra, Brazil.

English 2A Class List

Name	From
Michael Wong	
Anita Perez	Serra, Brazil
Jason Kim	
Joanne Reilly	Sydney, Australia
Alejandro Gonzalez	
Keiko Kubota	Tokyo, Japan
Deb Smith	London, England

3 Who's that?
STUDENT A

Ask and answer questions with Student B to complete the chart.

A: Who's that?
B: That's my mother.

Who?	sister	mother	
Name?	Margarita		
Age?	29		32
Married?	no		yes

4 That's Sarah.
STUDENT A

Take turns describing the people with Student B. Write the people's names.

A: This person is tall. She has blond hair and blue eyes.
B: That's Sarah.

Ken | | Sarah | | Lisa |

GRAMMAR TALK! **95**

5 Does he like Chinese food?
STUDENT A

Ask and answer questions with Student B to complete the chart.

A: Does Mina like soup?
B: Yes, she does.
A: Do Eric and Tomas like soup?
B: No, they don't.
A: Do you like soup?
B: Yes, I do.

	Mina	Eric and Tomas	Your partner
soup	yes	no	yes
fish	yes		
chicken		no	
steak	no		
French fries		yes	
cake	yes		
pie		no	
coffee		yes	
tea		yes	
pizza	no		
hamburgers	no		

6 Is he sleeping?
STUDENT A

Ask and answer questions with Student B about the people below.

A: Is Dan cleaning the kitchen?
B: No, he isn't. He's talking on the phone.

96

1 What's his first name?
STUDENT B

Ask and answer questions with Student A to complete Christopher's class information form.

A: What's the teacher's name?
B: Ruby Kelly.

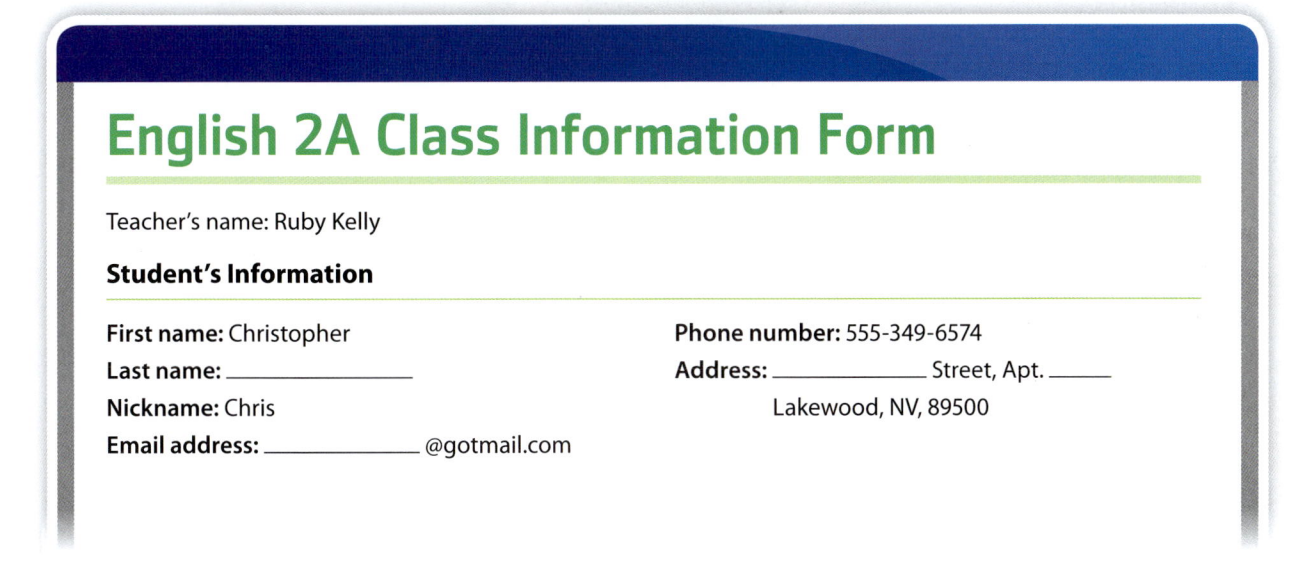

English 2A Class Information Form

Teacher's name: Ruby Kelly

Student's Information

First name: Christopher
Last name: _____
Nickname: Chris
Email address: _____ @gotmail.com

Phone number: 555-349-6574
Address: _____ Street, Apt. _____
Lakewood, NV, 89500

2 Where's he from?
STUDENT B

Ask and answer questions with Student A to complete the class list.

A: Where's Anita Perez from?
B: She's from Serra, Brazil.

English 2A Class List

Name	From
Michael Wong	Las Vegas, Nevada
Anita Perez	Serra, Brazil
Jason Kim	Seoul, South Korea
Joanne Reilly	
Alejandro Gonzalez	Zamora, Mexico
Keiko Kubota	
Deb Smith	

GRAMMAR TALK!

3 Who's that?
STUDENT B

Ask and answer questions with Student A to complete the chart.

A: Who's that?
B: That's my mother.

Who?		mother	brother
Name?		Theresa	Alejandro
Age?		54	
Married?		yes	

4 That's Sarah.
STUDENT B

Take turns describing the people with Student A. Write the people's names.

A: This person is tall. She has blond hair and blue eyes.
B: That's Sarah.

Clara   Sarah   John   Eduardo

98

5 Does he like Chinese food?
STUDENT B

Ask and answer questions with Student A to complete the chart.

A: Does Mina like soup?
B: Yes, she does.
A: Do Eric and Tomas like soup?
B: No, they don't.
A: Do you like soup?
B: Yes, I do.

	Mina	Eric and Tomas	Your partner
soup	yes	no	
fish		no	
chicken	no		
steak		yes	
French fries	no		
cake		yes	
pie	yes		
coffee	no		
tea	yes		
pizza		yes	
hamburgers		no	

6 Is he sleeping?
STUDENT B

Ask and answer questions with Student A about the people below.

A: Is Dan cleaning the kitchen?
B: No, he isn't. He's talking on the phone.

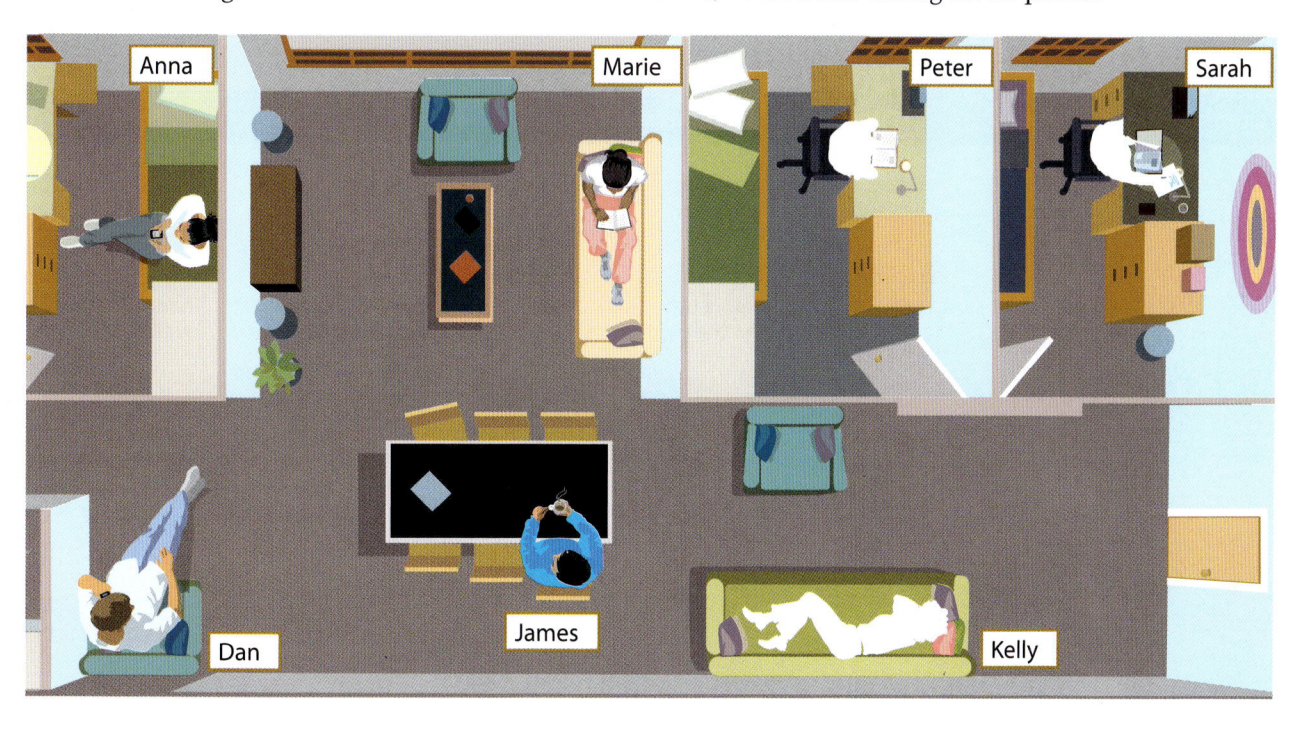

GRAMMAR TALK! 99

7 Is there a yard?
STUDENT A

Ask and answer questions with Student B about the house. Complete the sentences.

A: Are there any bedrooms on the first floor?   B: Yes, there's one bedroom on the first floor.

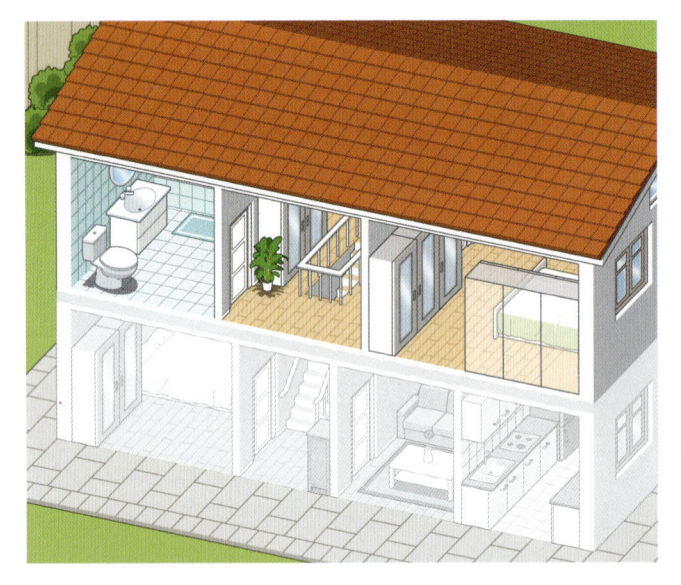

1. There _____ bedroom on the first floor.
2. There _____ closets in the bedroom.
3. There _____ bathroom on the first floor.
4. There _____ kitchen on the first floor.
5. There _____ dining room on the first floor.

8 What does he do on weekends?
STUDENT A

Ask and answer questions with Student B about Phillip's schedule. Ask five questions with *what, who, where, when,* and *how often*.

A: What does Philip do on Mondays?
B: He works out and studies.

A: How often does he work out?
B: He works out two times or three times a week.

FEBRUARY

Sunday	Monday	Tuesday	Wednesday	Thursday	Friday	Saturday
	1 *work out* ___ *study*	2 cook ___	3 work out at home	4 study at ___	5 work out at the gym	6 go to ___
7 play tennis	8 work out at ___	9 cook ___	10 work out at the gym	11 study ___	12 eat out with Mom and Dad	13 hang out with Ken
14	15 work out at ___	16 cook ___	17 work out at the gym	18 study at ___	19 go to a concert	20 go to the movies with ___
21	22 work out at ___	23 study ___	24 work out at the gym	25 play ___	26	27 hang out with Ken
28 go food shopping						

100

9 Can he swim?
STUDENT A

Ask and answer questions with Student B to complete Martin's camp counselor application.

A: Can Martin swim?   B: Yes, he can.

OAKDALE CAMP > CAMP COUNSELOR APPLICATION

Camp Counselor Application

Name: **Martin Silvestre**

Can you …?	Yes	No
swim	✓	
surf		✓
paddleboard	✓	
play volleyball		✓
play soccer	✓	
bike	✓	
play basketball		
play baseball		
do martial arts		
hike		

10 Is she going to move?
STUDENT A

Ask and answer questions with Student B to complete Luna's plans. Ask about the activities in the box.

| take a vacation | visit someone | take a class | rent an apartment |
| get a job | read | join a team | take piano lessons |

A: Is Luna going to take a vacation next fall?
B: Yes, she is. She's going to go to Florida.

Plans for Next Summer	Plans for Next Fall
get a job at the mall	_____
visit my friends Sara and Jane in Los Angeles	_____
take piano lessons	_____
take a martial arts class	_____
read three books	_____

GRAMMAR TALK! 101

11 Where is she going to go?
STUDENT A

Ask and answer questions with Student B to complete the email conversation.

A: What's Ella going to do on Friday night?
B: She's going to work.

To: jennifer.steiner@kgmail.com
From: ella.ang@kgmail.com
Subject: This weekend

Hi Jennifer,

Yes, I love baseball games! Let's go! I'm going to call you tomorrow evening.

Ella

From Jennifer Steiner:

Hey Ella!

I'm great! Yes, let's get together. I'm going to study on Friday night. I don't have any plans on Saturday. I'm just going to stay home and clean my apartment. I'm going to go to a baseball game on Sunday. Do you want to come?

Jennifer

From Ella Ang:

Hi Jennifer,

How is everything going? What are you doing this weekend? Let's get together. I'm going to ¹_____ on Friday night, and I'm going to visit ²_____ on Saturday. But I'm going to ³_____ on Sunday.

Ella

---

12 What did he do last Monday?
STUDENT A

Ask and answer questions with Student B to complete Jack's calendar.

A: What did Jack do last Monday morning?
B: He worked.

Sunday	Monday	Tuesday	Wednesday	Thursday	Friday	Saturday
1 morning: breakfast with Tomas	2 morning: _____	3 morning: drive to airport	4 morning: go to the beach	5 morning: visit _____	6 morning: _____	7 morning: _____
	evening: pack	evening: arrive in Cancun, Mexico	evening: have dinner with _____	evening:	evening: have dinner with Maria	evening: listen to music

102

7 Is there a yard?
STUDENT B

Ask and answer questions with Student A about the house. Complete the sentences.

A: Are there any bedrooms on the first floor?   B: Yes, there's one bedroom on the first floor.

1. There _____ bedroom on the second floor.
2. There _____ closets in the bedroom.
3. There _____ bathroom on the second floor.
4. There _____ closets in the bathroom.
5. There _____ closet in the hall.

8 What does he do on weekends?
STUDENT B

Ask and answer questions with Student A about Phillip's schedule. Ask five questions with *what*, *who*, *where*, *when*, and *how often*.

A: What does Philip do on Mondays?   A: How often does he work out?
B: He works out and studies.   B: He works out two times or three times a week.

			FEBRUARY			
Sunday	Monday	Tuesday	Wednesday	Thursday	Friday	Saturday
	1 work out study	2 cook dinner	3 work out at _____	4 study at the library	5 work out at _____	6 go to the movies
7 play _____	8 work out at the park	9 cook dinner	10 work out at _____	11 study at the library	12 eat out with _____	13 hang out with _____
14	15 work out at the park	16 cook dinner	17 work out at _____	18 study at the library	19 go to _____	20 go to the movies with Jay
21	22 work out at the park	23 study	24 work out at _____	25 play tennis	26	27 hang out with _____
28 go _____						

GRAMMAR TALK! 103

9 Can he swim?
STUDENT B

Ask and answer questions with Student A to complete Martin's camp counselor application.

A: Can Martin swim?   B: Yes, he can.

OAKDALE CAMP > CAMP COUNSELOR APPLICATION

Camp Counselor Application

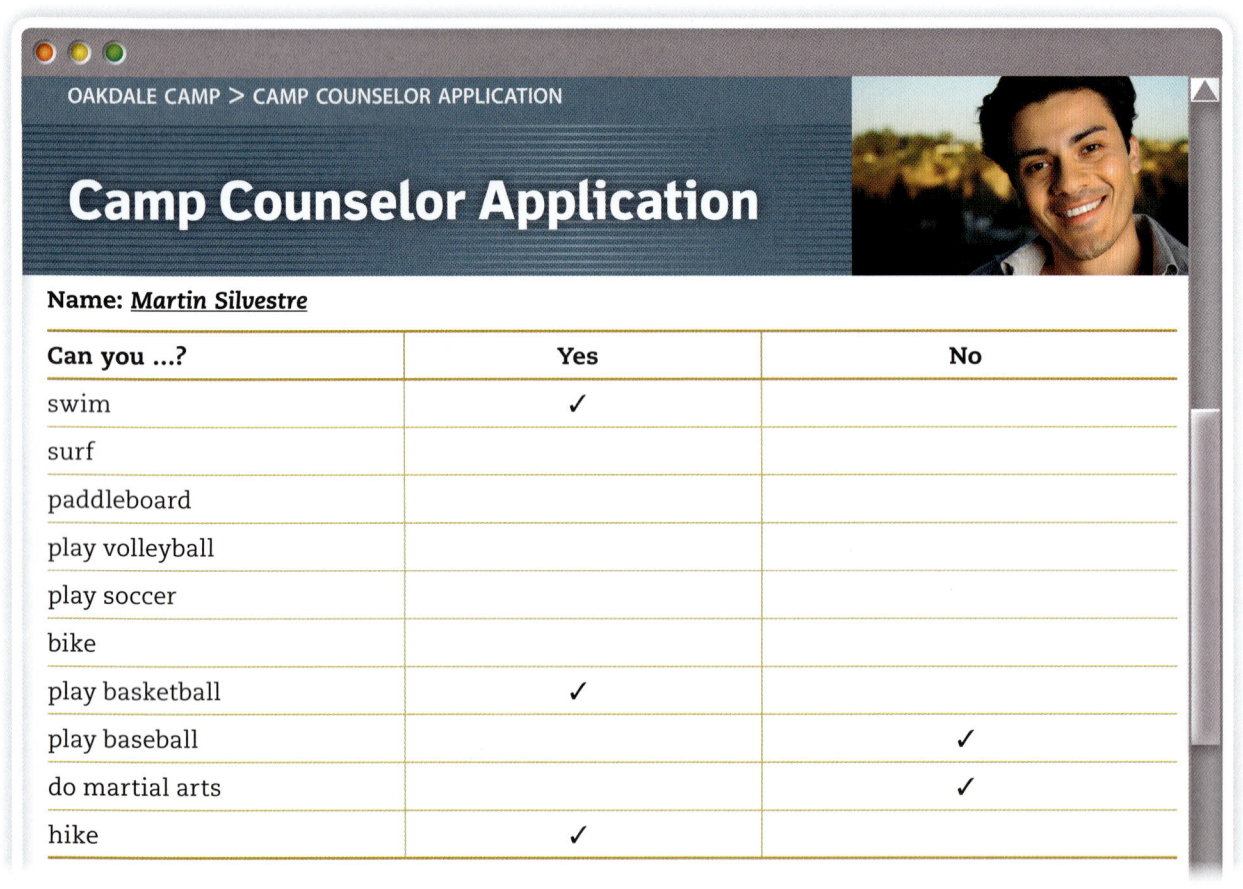

Name: *Martin Silvestre*

Can you …?	Yes	No
swim	✓	
surf		
paddleboard		
play volleyball		
play soccer		
bike		
play basketball	✓	
play baseball		✓
do martial arts		✓
hike	✓	

10 Is she going to move?
STUDENT B

Ask and answer questions with Student A to complete Luna's plans. Ask about the activities in the box.

| take a vacation | visit someone | take a class | rent an apartment |
| get a job | read | join a team | take piano lessons |

A: Is Luna going to take a vacation next fall?
B: Yes, she is. She's going to go to Florida.

Plans for Next Summer	Plans for Next Fall
_____	rent an apartment near school
_____	take a vacation for one week in Florida
_____	visit my cousin Michael
_____	join the basketball team
_____	get a job near school

104

11 Where is she going to go?
STUDENT B

Ask and answer questions with Student A to complete the email conversation.

A: What's Ella going to do on Friday night?
B: She's going to work.

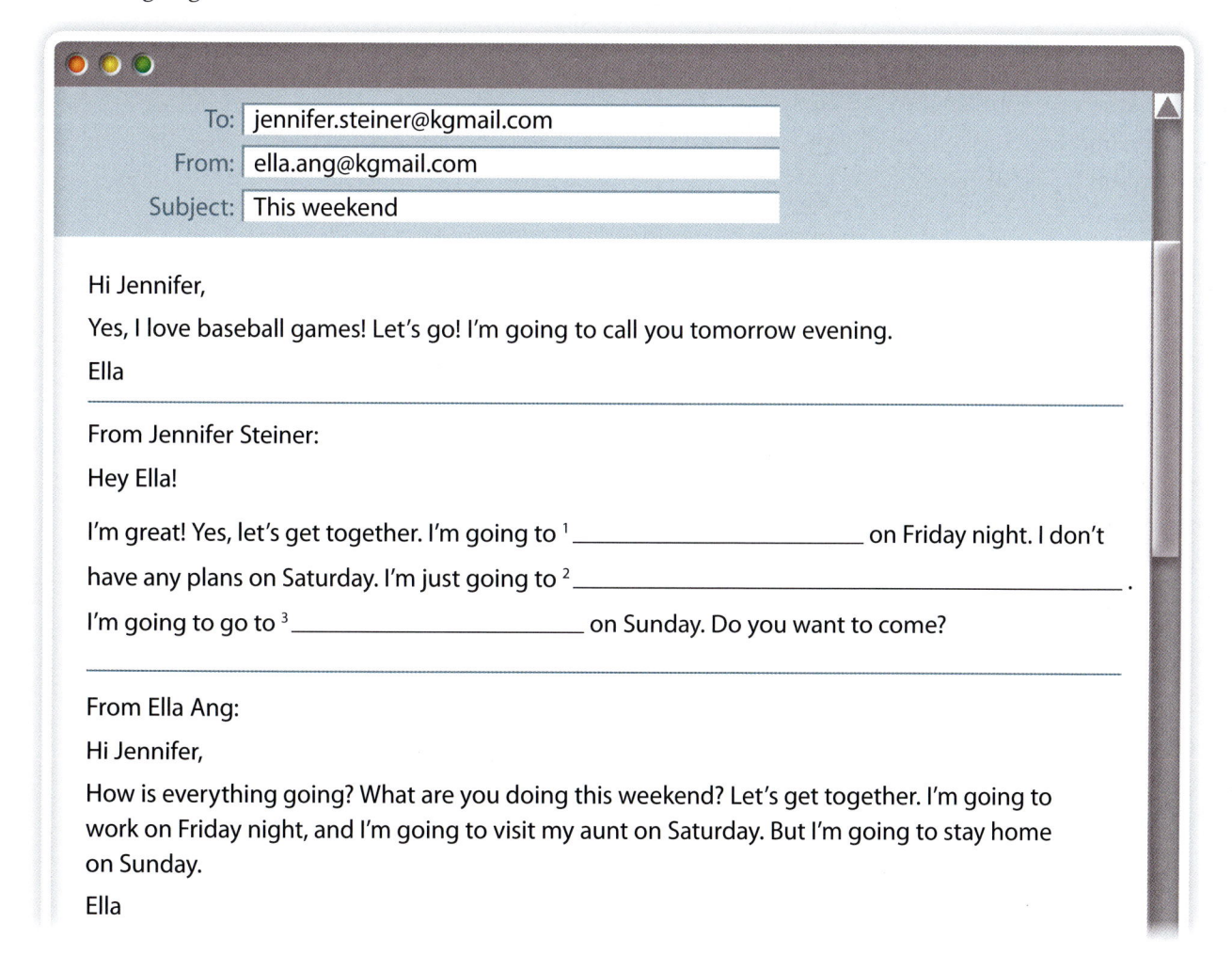

To: jennifer.steiner@kgmail.com
From: ella.ang@kgmail.com
Subject: This weekend

Hi Jennifer,

Yes, I love baseball games! Let's go! I'm going to call you tomorrow evening.

Ella

―――――――――――――――――――――――――――

From Jennifer Steiner:

Hey Ella!

I'm great! Yes, let's get together. I'm going to [1] _____ on Friday night. I don't have any plans on Saturday. I'm just going to [2] _____ . I'm going to go to [3] _____ on Sunday. Do you want to come?

―――――――――――――――――――――――――――

From Ella Ang:

Hi Jennifer,

How is everything going? What are you doing this weekend? Let's get together. I'm going to work on Friday night, and I'm going to visit my aunt on Saturday. But I'm going to stay home on Sunday.

Ella

12 What did he do last Monday?
STUDENT B

Ask and answer questions with Student A to complete Jack's calendar.

A: What did Jack do last Monday morning?
B: He worked.

Sunday	Monday	Tuesday	Wednesday	Thursday	Friday	Saturday
1 morning: breakfast with _____	2 morning: work	3 morning: drive to _____	4 morning: _____	5 morning: visit Mexico Park	6 morning: take surfing lessons	7 morning: go to the beach
	evening: pack	evening: arrive in _____	evening: have dinner with Tomas	evening: relax	evening: have dinner with Maria	evening: listen to _____

GRAMMAR TALK! 105

WORD LIST

Unit 1
VOCABULARY
name
nickname
first name
last name
address
apartment number
phone number
email address

USEFUL PHRASES
Could you repeat that?
Excuse me?

READING VOCABULARY
student
school
favorite
birthday
movies

Unit 2
VOCABULARY
Australia
Australian
Brazil
Brazilian
Vietnam
Vietnamese
Japan
Japanese
South Korea
South Korean
the United Kingdom
British
the United States
American
Mexico
Mexican

USEFUL PHRASES
Where are you from?
And you?
How about you?

READING VOCABULARY
introductions
student center
foods
dish
sign up

Unit 3
VOCABULARY
husband
wife
father
mother
son
daughter
brother
sister

READING VOCABULARY
family
picture
… years old
married
single

Unit 4
VOCABULARY
tall
black hair
brown eyes
short
blond hair
blue eyes
average height
brown hair
green eyes

USEFUL PHRASES
Well…
Um…

READING VOCABULARY
actor
twin
identical
character
TV shows

Unit 5
VOCABULARY
appetizers
soup
salad
sides
carrots
French fries
entrées
spaghetti
steak
chicken
fish
desserts
cake
pie
drinks
coffee
tea

USEFUL PHRASES
I like…
I love…
I hate…

READING VOCABULARY
reviews
restaurant
cheap
expensive
delicious

Unit 6
VOCABULARY
sleeping
studying
shopping
cooking dinner
going to work
taking a shower
texting
talking on the phone

READING VOCABULARY
mall
driving
shoes
test
history

Unit 7
VOCABULARY
living room
dining room
kitchen
bedroom
bathroom
yard
garage
hall
closet
balcony
stairs

USEFUL PHRASES
I like it because…

READING VOCABULARY
alike
walls
ceiling
strange
bubble

Unit 8
VOCABULARY
go to the movies
go shopping
eat out
work out at the gym
watch TV
listen to music
play video games
hang out with friends

USEFUL PHRASES
Oh?
That's interesting.

READING VOCABULARY
popular
million
computer games
every day
an hour or more

Unit 9
VOCABULARY
play volleyball
play soccer
play pool
do martial arts
do yoga
go biking
go snowboarding
go swimming

READING VOCABULARY
paddles
exercise
balance
workout
equipment

Unit 10
VOCABULARY
start school
get a job
take guitar lessons
graduate from high school
move
take a vacation
go on a date
celebrate a birthday

USEFUL PHRASES
Fabulous!
Wow!
Great!

READING VOCABULARY
months
best friends
save money
roommates
summer classes

Unit 11
VOCABULARY
watch a DVD
visit a museum
go away
spend time with my family
study for an exam
see friends
stay home and read
work

USEFUL PHRASES
Sure, I'd love to!
That sounds great!

READING VOCABULARY
exam
next week
garden
graduation ceremony
high school

Unit 12
VOCABULARY
went to Guam
arrived at the airport
rented a car
visited Tarzan Falls
took a lot of photos
ate delicious food
had a good time
came home

USEFUL PHRASES
That sounds like fun!
How exciting!

READING VOCABULARY
museums
walked around
sights
went shopping
next time

AUDIO AND VIDEO SCRIPTS

Unit 1
LISTENING page 2

1.
A: What's your address?
B: It's 22 Baker Street, London, United Kingdom.
2.
A: What's your name?
B: Susanna Chan.
3.
A: What's your phone number?
B: It's 555-323-6733.
4.
A: What's your apartment number?
B: It's apartment 3.
5.
A: What's your nickname?
B: Susie.
6.
A: What's your email address?
B: It's SChan33@coolmail.com

Unit 1
VIDEO page 6

N: Mohini Sule is in Malaysia. Today she is going to Kuala Gandah, an elephant sanctuary. Kuala Ganda is about one hundred and fifty kilometers from Kuala Lumpur, in the state of Pahang.
Mohini: Hi.
Guide: Welcome to Kuala Gandah.
Mohini: Thank you.
N: There are now only about 1,200 wild Asian elephants in Malaysia. At Kualah Gandah, people save elephants. Then they return some of the elephants to the wild.
Mohini: That's so cute! Have a hug. Elephant hug.
Guide: Yeah.
This is Abbot.
Mohini: Hello.
Guide: That's the naughty elephant.
Mohini: Look at her climbing around the tree there, that's great.
Guide: Why I say the naughty one, because she's very intelligent.
Mohini: Who's this one, Vetri?
Guide: This is Lucky Mala. Indian elephant.
N: Here at Kuala Gandah, people can walk with the elephants, feed them, and wash them. Elephants love water!
Mohini: Let's go to Cherry, the baby, shall we?
She's six years old. Ooh! Hi, sweetie, there you go.
She's hungry, as well. Yes!
This is Pyang. She's 33 years old. And, more food…
Ooh, one second, one second, can I put this in your mouth, Pyang?
Oooh!
You're beautiful.
N: Elephants are big, but they're gentle. They like people, and they are very smart.
Man: Shall we go now?
Mohini: Let's go!
Ready for a bumpy ride!
That means good job, good elephant. Good elephant. OK, I'll try it again. OK.
Guide: Try again.
Mohini: [in Malay]
No, that was not right. More from the belly.
Guide: [in Malay]
Mohini: [in Malay]
Please? If I say please, does that make it any different? OK, one more try, please do it for me this time, you ready?
Guide: [in Malay]
Mohini: Oh, you cutie. Can I just play with you all day? Can I take you home with me?

Unit 2
LISTENING page 8

1. My name is Kim. I'm from Vietnam.
2. I'm Marco. I'm from Brazil.
3. Her name's Linda. She's Mexican.
4. His name's John. He's from South Korea.

Unit 2
VIDEO page 12

N: São Paulo, Brazil, is the largest city in Latin America. It has a population of more than eleven million people.
People of many ethnicities live in São Paulo: Portuguese, Italian, Korean, Japanese, and many more.
São Paulo also has a lot of cars! All those cars create some jobs. Meet Ana Paula.
Ana Paula: My name is Ana Paula, and I'm a motorgirl.
N: Ana Paula delivers things all over the city.
Ana Paula: Good morning. How's everything?
Everything OK?
Thanks. Bye bye.
N: São Paulo is a big and busy city, but for people like Ana Paula, it's a great place to work.
On the other side of the world is another big city. Like São Paulo, it has a population of about eleven million people. Let's meet two of those people.
Cho Sung-hoon: My name is Cho Sung-hoon. I'm South Korean. I live in Seoul, and I work here at the fish market. I'm an auctioneer.
N: It is 6:00 in the morning, and the workers at the fish market are already busy. This fish market is open 24 hours a day. It is very big – the size of ten soccer fields.
Yoon Soo-yeon: My name is Yoon Soo-yeon. I'm a waiter here at Soo Yeon San Bang Tea House. The people of Seoul come here for a little bit of Korean tradition.
Young people come here to learn about the traditions.
Older people come here to talk with friends.
N: Seoul: A city where the old lives next to the new.

Unit 3
LISTENING page 14
1. Marcus isn't my friend. He's my brother.
2. Sara and Michelle are my sisters. They're not my friends.
3. Kim is my mother. She isn't my teacher.
4. Medina is my wife. She isn't my sister.
5. Carlos is my husband. He's not my brother.

Unit 3
VIDEO page 18
I: How many hats do you have?
Pace: One, two, three, four, five, six… a lot.
I: You have a lot.
N: Pace Hutchinson is ten years old. He has a typical room — he has a lot of hats, some toy motorcycles, and a coin collection.
Pace: Steel pennies…
N: But Pace is not a typical boy. He lives in an amusement park. It has twenty-eight rides, a lot of games, and even a water park! Pace's grandparents own the amusement park called Funtown Splashtown U.S.A. His grandfather, Ken Cormier, started the amusement park 53 years ago.
Violet: Popsicles!
N: Ken's wife, Violet, also works at the park.
Pace's mother has five brothers and sisters. Four of them work at the park, and two of them live there, too.
Pace's mother and father both work at the park. His mother, Kimberly, works in sales. Her husband, Cory, is a manager at the water park.
Cory: How's the water, Anton? Good?
N: Pace also works at the park. He looks for coins in the water. He finds about twenty dollars every week!
Pace loves the amusement park. His favorite ride is Dragon's Descent. It is two hundred and twenty feet high.
I: So this is your favorite?
Pace: Yeah.
N: This is Pace's four hundred and ninety-ninth time on the ride.
Pace: If I don't come back, give Harry all my video games!
N: When Pace grows up, he wants to work at the park with his family. But for now, he's just having fun.
I: Oh! How's my hair?
Pace: Pretty good.
I: Yours is pretty good, too.

Unit 4
LISTENING page 22
1.
A: Jill, tell me about your sister.
B: Well, her name's Kelly. She has beautiful black hair.
2.
A: Does your brother Michael have blue eyes?
B: No, he doesn't. He has brown eyes.
3.
A: Is Ella tall?
B: No, she isn't. She's short.
4.
A: Does your friend Robert have blue eyes?
B: Yes, he does.

Unit 4
VIDEO page 26
N: Hair. Your hairstyle can show people who you are. You can style it in many different ways. You can have long or short hair. You can curl it or dye it, decorate it or shave it all off. If you're a man, you can have a beard or a mustache. A hairstyle can show that you are part of a group. The Tunda people of southern India have long curls. The Hama people of Ethiopia wear curls, and they dye their hair brown. The Masai people of Kenya have many different hairstyles. When boys are twelve, they shave their hair off. On special days, they paint their hair red. Hair strands have different shapes. African hair strands are oval. African hair is very curly. Asian hair strands are round. Asian hair is very straight. Asian women sometimes wear their hair in a bun or braids. Caucasian hair is halfway between oval and round. Caucasian people style their hair in many different ways. When people get older, their hair becomes gray. Men often lose their hair. Some men wear wigs. Wigs are sometimes fun and fashionable. Hairstyles are always changing.
Look at these hairstyles of the 1950s…
The 1960s…
The 1970s …
The 1980s…
And today.
With your hairstyle, you can show the world who you are.

Unit 5
LISTENING page 28
A: Are you ready to order?
B: Yes, I am.
A: Can I get you an appetizer?
B: Yes, please. The house salad.
A: OK. And for your entrée?
B: Chicken with a side of carrots, please.
A: Anything to drink?
B: Coffee, please.
A: And for dessert? We have carrot cake and pie.
B: Hmmm, no dessert for me, thank you.

Unit 5
VIDEO page 32
N: People in Hong Kong love food. In fact, many people in Hong Kong eat five meals a day! Fiona Xie is in Hong Kong to learn about the wonderful food here. And she is very hungry! The Causeway Bay market sells fruits and vegetables. It also has a lot of Cantonese food.
Fiona: Whoa! It's alive!
N: Fiona is having lunch with Walter Kei today.
Fiona: Hi, Walter.
Walter: Hi, Fiona.
Fiona: Hi.
N: Walter is a famous food critic. He knows where to find great Cantonese food. First, they're going to a food court.
Fiona: Ah, I can smell the food already. Yes, food, glorious food!
N: The food court has many different kinds of Cantonese food. And it's very cheap!

Fiona: You know, when people come to Hong Kong, what do they have to try, definitely have to try?
Walter: Uh, I think wonton noodles.
Fiona: Wonton noodles.
Walter: Roast duck.
Fiona: Roast duck. Which is this. Whoa, look at that! And what's the third thing that they have to try?
Walter: And dim sum.
Fiona: Dim sum, wonton noodles, and roast duck. Mmm…
N: Now they're going to Walter's favorite restaurant.
Fiona: Welcome to Maxim's Palace, Hong Kong's most famous dim sum restaurant.
N: They serve food on a cart. You point to the food you want.
Fiona: Hello!
N: They are going into the kitchen to learn how to make dim sum.
Fiona: Hi!
Chef: Hi.
Walter: This is my friend, Fiona.
Fiona: Hello!
Chef: Hi.
Fiona: Nice to meet you!
Walter: His nickname is, uh, Cheung Fun Wong.
N: Cooking rice noodle rolls is difficult, but Cheung Fun Wong makes it look easy.
Fiona: Whoa!
Chef: Yeah, it's already done.
Fiona: Oh, look at that, look at that, it's all stuck to it! It's a skill! Check this out!
Chef: Eee-yah!
N: The restaurant serves two hundred kinds of dim sum. This is just one of those. To pay for her dim sum, Fiona is working at the restaurant.
Fiona: Gwat! How do you spell Gwat? A little cart, and I got a little apron. I'm ready to rock and roll. Hong Kong, here I come!

Unit 6

LISTENING page 34

1. Ana's shopping.
2. The baby's sleeping.
3. They're cooking dinner.
4. Pam's studying.

Unit 6

VIDEO page 38

N: There is something new at the Detroit Medical Center. Robots are visiting patients!
Doctor: You been coughing for a few days now?
Patient: Yeah.
Doctor: OK.
N: The hospital has ten of these robots. They help many people at the hospital. The robots don't work alone. A doctor is always helping through the Internet.
Woman: How do you feel about, um, talking to a robot instead of a doctor?
Doctor: He *is* talking to a doctor, Elizabeth!
Woman: The beauty of it is really quite simple. It allows doctors to be several places at once. They can be in their office, or even at home, overlooking charts and x-rays, and be at the patient's bedside at the same time.
N: Doctors log on to the robot, and visit patients in the hospital. Right now, Dr. Santucci is at home, and the hospital needs him.
Doctor: Beautiful.
Woman: So they would page you at home.
Doctor: Sure.
Woman: You'd stop cooking dinner.
Doctor: Yeah.
Woman: And you'd come over and check in on a patient.
Doctor: Right, exactly right.
N: Doctor Santucci is controlling the robot from half an hour away. He can talk to other doctors before he talks to patients. Many doctors and patients like the robots. Does this patient like the robots?
Patient: Yeah.
Woman: The way we're going?
N: Surgeon Dr. Michael Klein says the robots also help a patient see another doctor in another city.
Dr. Klein: And this is a way that we can actually bring expert care to, uh, to people's bedsides.
N: The robots will not make doctors go away from hospitals, only help them. There is just one problem with the robots.
Doctor: Pardon me, could I ask you to plug me in?
Woman: OK.
N: They need power.

Unit 6

PRESENTING page 39

On weekday mornings, I usually get up at 6:00. I check my texts, and then I go for a walk in the park. After that I take a shower. At about 7:30 I have breakfast, usually toast and coffee. At 8:00 I take the subway to work. I start work at 9:00. So that's my morning: texts, a walk, a shower, the subway, and work.

Unit 7
LISTENING page 42
1.
- A: Do you like your new apartment, Zai?
- B: Oh, I love it! It's really big.
- A: Is the bedroom big?
- B: It has *two* bedrooms. And it has a living room, a big kitchen, and a nice bathroom.

2.
- A: How's your new apartment, Jessica?
- B: Well, it's cute, but it's really small. It has only one room and a bathroom.
- A: Really? You don't have a bedroom?
- B: No, I sleep in the living room.

3.
- A: Do you like your new apartment, Jake?
- B: Not really. It's too small.
- A: Really? It's too small?
- B: Yeah. I have one bedroom, a small kitchen, a living room, and a small bathroom.

Unit 7
VIDEO page 46
Jay: Do you guys want to come on in?
N: Jay Schafer's house is small, really, really small. It's tiny. It has a tiny bedroom. There's a closet and some shelves.
Jay: Take a look at the kitchen, and the bathroom. And there's a lot of storage here, too. I have a flush toilet.
N: Tiny houses are becoming more popular these days. Why? Well, first, they're cheap.
Elizabeth Randol: I think they're amazing.
N: Right now Elizabeth Randol lives in an average size house, but she wants to buy a tiny house.
Elizabeth: You buy the house, no mortgage and no utilities. So any money that you make goes right into your pocket.
N: Schafer drives around the country with his tiny house. He teaches people about building small houses. When he stops, a lot of people want to see the house.
Jim: You're kind of a rock star.
Jay: Uh, I would like to think so. I mean, it's, you know, in a tiny way.
Man in car: Nice house.
Jay: Thank you.
N: There aren't many tiny houses in the United States. But Jay wants to change that. Tiny houses are *already* popular in Japan. Small houses often have interesting architecture. Some, like this one, are very narrow. This tiny house has a narrow hall. It has a small indoor garden. There's one bathroom with a shower. Because of these plants, people can't see you when you're in the bathroom. The house has one small bedroom… *very* small! In this small house, the table doesn't have legs. Big windows give the house a lot of light.
Man: There aren't any closets, so we don't have many things.
N: Tiny houses are a great way to have a simple and inexpensive life.

PRESENTING page 47
My dream house is in the mountains. It's huge! There are six bedrooms and six bathrooms. A lot of friends can visit me on the weekends. It has an enormous living room and dining room. The kitchen has two stoves and two refrigerators. In the basement, there's a movie theater. There's a big swimming pool behind the house.

Unit 8
LISTENING page 48
1.
- A: Do you like to go to the movies?
- B: Yes! I go to the movies about once a week.

2.
- A: Do you work out at the gym?
- B: Ugh, no. I don't like gyms.

3.
- A: Do you like to watch TV?
- B: Not really. I don't even have a television.

4.
- A: Do you like to play video games?
- B: I play video games all the time! Come over tonight. Let's play a game together!

Unit 8
VIDEO page 52
N: New York City. It's a great place to go shopping, to eat out, to go for a walk in the park, and to play chess.
Russ: My name is Russ Makofsky. We're in the Village Chess Shop in Greenwich Village, New York. And this neighborhood is known as the chess capital of the world.
N: Over seventy percent of the chess players in the United States live in New York. The number of chess players grows by two hundred percent every year. It is a part of New York's street culture. There are two kinds of chess players in New York. There are serious, professional chess players. They want to be champions. And then, there are street chess players.
Russ: There's about, probably, I'd say, five to seven different parks and location throughout New York City that are known for their street chess.
N: Russ is director of Chess NYC. It has summer chess camps for young students. Children love the camp. They come every day in the summer. They arrive at 8:45 in the morning. The kids play chess all morning, and then they go out for pizza. In the afternoon, the children play more chess. Then they play in the fountain at Washington Square Park. Today, Justice Williams is helping at the camp. He's a 14-year-old chess player. He started playing when he was eight, and now he's a national master.
Justice: When I was in third grade, my mom wanted me to pick up an activity and instead of choosing something like basketball she wanted me to try something different, so she put me in a chess program, and that's how I got started.
N: Justice is now famous. He's on the cover of magazines, and he was even in a movie about young chess players. Young or old, if you love chess, Greenwich Village is the place to be!

Unit 8
PRESENTING page 53
In our class, twenty-two percent of students go to the movies one to four times a week. Thirty-five percent go to the movies once or twice a month. Forty percent go one to four times a year. And two percent never go to the movies. Maybe they like to watch movies at home.

Unit 9
LISTENING page 54

1.
A: What do you do for exercise, Tara?
B: Well, I'm taking a martial arts class.
A: Really? Martial arts?
B: Yeah, I go to class once a week.

2.
A: Do you like sports, John?
B: Sure. I like to play volleyball.
A: Really? How often do you play?
B: My team practices twice a week.

3.
A: What sports do you like, Jake?
B: Well, I do a lot of biking.
A: Oh, yeah?
B: Yeah, I bike to work every day.

4.
A: Do you like soccer, Rose?
B: Yes, I do. I like it very much.
A: How often do you play?
B: Oh, I never play soccer. I watch it on TV.

5.
A: Do you get much exercise, Dave?
B: Not too much. But I like swimming.
A: How often do you go swimming?
B: Not very often. I go about once a month.

Unit 9
VIDEO page 58

N: Can you surf? Can you snowboard? Then you can brush board. Brush boarding is an exciting new sport. You can do it in any kind of weather, any time of year. You can do it without water or snow. It looks easy, but it's pretty difficult. People of any age can learn to brush board, even young children.

I: You're brilliant! Tell us what it was like.

Girl: Fun.

Boy: Absolutely tiring.

Teenage boy: And if you can't swim, this is a great alternative for surfboarding.

Man: You want to put your feet right on the edge. Your toes are just on the edge. You want to keep digging your toes in. Knees bent. And you're going to put your hand out in front of you.

N: Older people can learn to brush board, too. To brush board, you need good balance. You also need a lot of practice. If you do fall, it doesn't hurt, and you won't get wet.

Kyle: It's never going to be like surfing, it's never going to be snowboarding, but it will get you fit and ready so when you have time to go do that chosen sport, you'll be, you'll be good to go.

N: Brush boarding: It's a great workout. And it's a lot of fun!

Unit 10
LISTENING page 62

1. My husband and I are going to move next weekend.
2. I'm so happy for my sister. She's going to graduate from high school next week.
3. My little brother is going to start school next month.
4. My birthday is next Saturday. I'm going to go out and celebrate with friends.

Unit 10
VIDEO page 66

N: Antonia is a student. She's going to graduate from high school next month. Her friends are shopping for furniture for college, but Antonia is preparing to travel.

Antonia: I'm going to Madrid, where I'll take Spanish lessons. I'm going to Berlin, where I'm going to take German lessons. And then I'm probably going to travel on my own a little bit, um, around Central and Eastern Europe. Isn't that cool?

N: Antonia spent a summer in France. After that summer, she decided to travel again after high school.

Taking a year off between high school and college can help students in the future. According to a survey of 350 students, 55% said taking a year off helped their grades. 57% said their gap year helped them find a job after they graduated from college. Ron Lieber is the co-author of *Taking Time Off*. He says that it's important to have a plan for your gap year.

Ron: Taking time off is… is almost like school in the sense that you need to plan every day, every month, you need a lesson plan, you need a syllabus.

N: After Trudy Goodman finished high school, she wanted a break from studying.

Trudy: I was at the same school for ten years. I was ready for a different type of challenge.

N: So Trudy took a gap year. She moved to Boston, and worked with children at schools and in their neighborhoods. After one year, Trudy was ready to start college.

Trudy: I had some experiences to share, um, as examples in classes, that I never would have had, um, had I not had this experience.

Unit 11
LISTENING page 68

1.
A: Are you going to do anything special this weekend?
B: I'm going to study for an exam.
A: Are you going to study alone?
B: No. I'm going to study with some friends.

2.
A: What are your plans for the weekend?
B: I'm going to go out to dinner on Saturday.
A: Who are you going to go with?
B: With my friends.
A: That's nice.

3.
A: What are you and Sarah going to do this weekend?
B: Nothing special. I think we're going to watch a lot of TV.
A: Are you going to watch the baseball game on Sunday?
B: Oh, yeah! Sarah and I love baseball!

4.
A: What are your plans for the weekend?
B: I'm going to spend some time with my family.
A: Are you going to stay home?
B: Not all weekend. We're going to eat out on Saturday.

Unit 11
VIDEO page 72

N: This weekend, Mohini Sule is visiting the island of Bali. She's going to go scuba diving.
Mohini: Hi, how you doing?
Peter: Fine. Ready for some diving?
Mohini: I am indeed. Let's go.
N: Mohini is going to scuba dive at a tropical reef. She's going to see wildlife that is in danger from both people and nature. With her is divemaster, Peter.
Mohini: Menjangan is a national park, isn't it?
Peter: It is, it is. Yeah, it's like a national park. You have deers on that island as well.
N: They are going to take a boat from the western seaport of Gilimanuk. To get there, they're driving through the Bali Barat National Park.
Peter: We're here.
Mohini: This is beautiful.
N: Many dive boats leave from Gilimanuk seaport. Today, they're going on a dive with Peter's friend, Chip.
Mohini: Hi!
N: Chip is an expert scuba diver. Here they are.
Menjangan is a very popular place for diving. It's a good place for expert divers, or beginners, like Mohini.
Mohini: The moment has arrived to take my first dive.
N: The water is very clear here. Mohini is getting ready for her first dive.
Man: There we go.
N: It's easy to learn to scuba dive. Now, the underwater adventure begins! They are going to dive down to about ten meters. There are a lot of fish near the reef. The fish are beautiful, and so colorful.
Mohini: That was so awesome! We actually went down to ten meters, was it?
Peter: Yeah, ten point two it is.
N: It was a wonderful day in a beautiful place.

Unit 12
LISTENING page 74

1.
A: Did you have a good vacation?
B: I had a great vacation!
A: Where did you go?
B: I went to Thailand.
2.
A: Did you have a good time on your vacation?
B: Not bad.
A: Where did you go?
B: Oh, I didn't go away. I just stayed home and relaxed.
3.
A: When did you get back from vacation?
B: Last week.
A: Did you go to the beach?
B: No, not this time. I visited relatives in California.
A: Did you have a good time?
B: Not really. Everyone got sick.
4.
A: What did you do on your vacation?
B: I went snowboarding.
A: Did you have a good time?
B: Yeah. I had an amazing time!

Unit 12
VIDEO page 78

N: Welcome to Sydney. Millions of tourists come here each year for art, the ocean, and the food. Carmen has to find three things in Sydney and her boss will text them to Carmen, because…
Carmen: Today we're going local! First challenge: Find the best meat pie in Sydney.
Are you a tourist or a local?
Man: [walks by]
I think that means tourist.
Hi there. Are you a tourist or a local?
Woman: I'm from Brisbane.
Carmen: Tourist.
N: Carmen talked to a hairdresser.
Carmen: Sorry to interrupt. I'm trying to find Sydney's best meat pie.
Man: Uh, Bourke Street Bakery.
Carmen: This must be the right place. Check out all the people. Wow. Smells amazing. Your pie looks amazing. Would you mind if I had just a wee taste?
Man: I guess.
Carmen: Thanks. Oh, wow. So good.
Excuse me, can I have a pie?
Mmmm…
Next challenge: Find a beach that only locals know about. Where's a beach that only local Sydney people go to?
Man: Oh, that's very difficult. Umm… There's a beach near Tamarama.
Carmen: Hi! Hi. You going to Tamarama?
Wow!
Are you a local?
Next challenge: Watch a local game.
So we traveled about half an hour west of Sydney to get here to Sydney Olympic Park. Look at all these people! There's like 30,000 people here! What an atmosphere! Hope I can find a seat.
How are the Giants doing on their first game out?
Fan: Excellent. Showing a lot of spunk.

AUDIO AND VIDEO SCRIPTS 113

OXFORD
UNIVERSITY PRESS

198 Madison Avenue
New York, NY 10016 USA

Great Clarendon Street, Oxford, ox2 6DP, United Kingdom

Oxford University Press is a department of the University of Oxford.
It furthers the University's objective of excellence in research, scholarship,
and education by publishing worldwide. Oxford is a registered trade
mark of Oxford University Press in the UK and in certain other countries

© Oxford University Press 2014

The moral rights of the author have been asserted

First published in 2014

2018 2017 2016 2015

10 9 8 7 6 5 4 3

No unauthorized photocopying

All rights reserved. No part of this publication may be reproduced, stored in a retrieval system, or transmitted, in any form or by any means, without the prior permission in writing of Oxford University Press, or as expressly permitted by law, by licence or under terms agreed with the appropriate reprographics rights organization. Enquiries concerning reproduction outside the scope of the above should be sent to the ELT Rights Department, Oxford University Press, at the address above

You must not circulate this work in any other form and you must impose this same condition on any acquirer

Links to third party websites are provided by Oxford in good faith and for information only. Oxford disclaims any responsibility for the materials contained in any third party website referenced in this work

Director, ELT New York: Laura Pearson
Executive Publishing Manager: Erik Gundersen
Publisher, Adult Coursebooks: Louisa van Houten
Managing Editor: Tracey Gibbins
Senior Development Editor: Cristina Zurawski
Executive Art and Design Manager: Maj-Britt Hagsted
Content Production Manager: Julie Armstrong
Image Manager: Trisha Masterson
Production Coordinator: Brad Tucker

ISBN: 978 0 19 460307 2 STUDENT BOOK (PACK COMPONENT)
ISBN: 978 0 19 460311 9 STUDENT BOOK (PACK)
ISBN: 978 0 19 460367 6 ONLINE PRACTICE (PACK COMPONENT)

Printed in China

This book is printed on paper from certified and well-managed sources

ACKNOWLEDGEMENTS

Illustrations by: Debbie Lofaso, Cover Illustration; 5W Infographics, pg. 2, 6, 7, 28, 32, 38, 42, 44, 46, 47, 58, 66, 72, 78, 100, 103; Joe Taylor. Pg. 14, 22, 24, 26, 74, 95, 96, 98, 99.

We would also like to thank the following for permission to reproduce the following photographs: "Tip" presenters used throughout the book: Yuri Arcurs/Alamy; MANDY GODBEHEAR /Alamy; Jacob Yuri Wackerhausen /Tetra Images/Corbis; violetblue /shutterstock.com. Interior, Robin Skjoldborg / Getty Images, pg. 3; Robin Skjoldborg / Getty Images, pg. 4; Michael DeLeon / Getty Images, pg. 4; Goodluz / Shutterstock, pg. 4; © Ocean / Corbis, pg. 4; Alejandro Rivera/ Getty Images, pg. 4; © blickwinkel / Alamy, pg. 4; © Jade / Blend Images / Corbis, pg. 5; © AF archive / Alamy, pg. 7; amorfati.art / Shutterstock, pg. 8; pdesign / Shutterstock, pg. 8; Graphi-Ogre / OUP, pg. 8; Graphi-Ogre / OUP, pg. 8; Graphi-Ogre / OUP, pg. 8; Graphi-Ogre / OUP, pg. 8; Graphi-Ogre / OUP, pg. 8; Graphi-Ogre / OUP, pg. 8; Graphi-Ogre / OUP, pg. 8; Graphi-Ogre / OUP, pg. 8; pdesign / Shutterstock, pg. 8; Compassionate Eye Foundation / Chris Ryan / Getty Images, pg. 9; quavondo / Getty Images, pg. 10; Graphi-Ogre / OUP, pg. 10; © Beau Lark / Corbis, pg. 10; Graphi-Ogre / OUP, pg. 10; PhotoTalk / Getty Images, pg. 10; Graphi-Ogre / OUP, pg. 10; © Holger Scheibe / Corbis, pg. 10; amorfati.art / Shutterstock, pg. 10; MIXA / Getty Images, pg. 10; Graphi-Ogre / OUP, pg. 10; © Blue Images / Corbis, pg. 10; pdesign / Shutterstock, pg. 10; fotostorm / iStockphoto, pg. 10; Graphi-Ogre / OUP, pg. 10; Ju-Lee / iStockphoto, pg. 11; Debbi Smirnoff / Getty Images, pg. 11; Maria Komar / Shutterstock, pg. 11; © Andre Seale / Robert Harding Specialist Stock / Corbis, pg. 12; © Pablo Rivera / Golden Pixels LLC / Corbis, pg. 13; © Wavebreak Media Ltd. / Corbis, pg. 13; Image Source / Getty Images, pg. 13; © IMAGEMORE1 / Imagemore Co., Ltd. / Corbis, pg. 15; © Drew Myers / Corbis, pg. 16; Fuse / Getty Images, pg. 16; © Dean Pictures / Corbis, pg. 16; Andrew Rich / Getty Images, pg. 16; © i love images / Fitness / Alamy, pg. 16; Inti St Clair / Getty Images, pg. 16; XiXinXing / Getty Images, pg. 16; Shelly Perry / Getty Images, pg. 17; Jessica Peterson / Getty Images, pg. 17; © Jeff Greenberg 2 of 6 / Alamy, pg. 18; Monkey Business Images / Shutterstock, pg. 19; szefei / Shutterstock, pg. 19; Tarick Foteh / Getty Images, pg. 21; David Lees / Getty Images, pg. 21; nyul / iStockphoto, pg. 23; Josiah Kamau / Getty Images, pg. 25; Gilbert Carrasquillo / Getty Images, pg. 25; Carlo Allegri / Getty Images, pg. 26; © Mark Bourdillon / Alamy, pg. 27; Jordan Siemens / Getty Images, pg. 29; © Stuart Monk / Alamy, pg. 30; © Viktor Fischer / Alamy, pg. 30; Maria Komar / Shutterstock, pg. 30; © Island Images / Alamy, pg. 30; milanfoto / Getty Images, pg. 30; Fotofermer / Shutterstock, pg. 30; Erkki Makkonen / Getty Images, pg. 30; LWA / Sharie Kennedy / Getty Images, pg. 31; racorn / Shutterstock, pg. 31; 3bugsmom / iStockphoto, pg. 31; © Jeremy Woodhouse / Spaces Images / Corbis, pg. 33; Tetra Images / Getty Images, pg. 34; © Image Source Plus / Alamy, pg. 34; © MBI / Alamy, pg. 34; © Agencja FREE / Alamy, pg. 34; Alexandr Dubovitskiy / iStockphoto, pg. 34; vitapix / iStockphoto, pg. 34; Peathegee Inc / Getty Images, pg. 34; Lane Oatey / Getty Images, pg. 34; © Andres Rodriguez / Alamy, pg. 34; bluehill75 / iStockphoto, pg. 34; Alberto Pomares / Getty Images, pg. 34; © MBI / Alamy, pg. 34; © Robyn Breen Shinn / Corbis, pg. 35; Squaredpixels / Getty Images, pg. 36; Hybrid Images / Getty Images, pg. 36; Odua Images / Shutterstock, pg. 36; Compassionate Eye Foundation / Chris Ryan / Getty Images, pg. 36; Fuse / Getty Images, pg. 36; Miroslav Georgijevic / Getty Images, pg. 36; Ariel Skelley / Getty Images, pg. 36; Goodluz / Shutterstock, pg. 37; PhotoTalk / Getty Images, pg. 37; stefanolunardi / Shutterstock, pg. 39; Jonathan Downey / Getty Images, pg. 41; © Ocean / Corbis, pg. 43; © Splash News / Corbis, pg. 45; © George Sheldon / Alamy, pg. 45; © Q-Images / Alamy, pg. 45; uniquely india / Getty Images, pg. 48; PhotoTalk / Getty Images, pg. 48; © Guy Cali / Corbis, pg. 48; Derek Latta / Getty Images, pg. 48; OJO Images / Getty Images, pg. 48; Jacom Stephens / Getty Images, pg. 48; webphotographeer / Getty Images, pg. 48; Fabrice LEROUGE / Getty Images, pg. 48; poba / Getty Images, pg. 49; PhotoTalk / Getty Images, pg. 50; Derek Latta / Getty Images, pg. 50; OJO Images / Getty Images, pg. 50; webphotographeer / Getty Images, pg. 50; © Guy Cali / Corbis, pg. 50; Fabrice LEROUGE / Getty Images, pg. 50; Jacom Stephens / Getty Images, pg. 50; © asiaselects / Corbis, pg. 51; littleny / Shutterstock, pg. 52; Steve Debenport / iStockphoto, pg. 53; © Prisma Bildagentur AG / Alamy, pg. 54; © Mika / Corbis, pg. 54; © Ruslan Kokarev / Alamy, pg. 54; Liane Cary / Getty Images, pg. 54; Hero Images / Getty Images, pg. 54; GlobalStock / Getty Images, pg. 54; © Cultura RM / Alamy, pg. 54; © Peter Phipp / Travelshots.com / Alamy, pg. 54; John Rensten / Getty Images, pg. 55; Hybrid Images / Getty Images, pg. 56; © Prisma Bildagentur AG / Alamy, pg. 56; © Cultura RM / Alamy, pg. 56; © Peter Phipp / Travelshots.com / Alamy, pg. 56; © Ruslan Kokarev / Alamy, pg. 56; © Mika / Corbis, pg. 56; Liane Cary / Getty Images, pg. 56; Blend Images - Erik Isakson / Getty Images, pg. 57; © ZUMA Press, Inc. / Alamy, pg. 59; © Tom Stewart / CORBIS, pg. 59; technotr / iStockphoto, pg. 59; Yuri Arcurs / Getty Images, pg. 61; Steve Debenport / Getty Images, pg. 62; Sportstock / Getty Images, pg. 62; Jupiterimages / Getty Images, pg. 62; © Samantha Mitchell / Corbis, pg. 62; YinYang / Getty Images, pg. 62; Abel Mitja Varela / Getty Images, pg. 62; Mike Kemp / Getty Images, pg. 62; Cavan Images / Getty Images, pg. 62; © Ocean / Corbis, pg. 62; Blend Images Jon Feingersh / Getty Images, pg. 62; Purestock / Getty Images, pg. 62; damircudic / iStockphoto, pg. 62; M Swiet Productions / Getty Images, pg. 63; luminaimages / Shutterstock, pg. 64; Abel Mitja Varela / Getty Images, pg. 64; Photolyric / iStockphoto, pg. 64; Stuart Jenner / Shutterstock, pg. 64; Steve Debenport / iStockphoto, pg. 64; © Patrik Giardino / Corbis, pg. 64; monkeybusinessimages / iStockphoto, pg. 64; zhang bo / Getty Images, pg. 65; © Andres Rodriguez / Alamy, pg. 65; oliale72 / Getty Images, pg. 65; Feng Wei Photography / Getty Images, pg. 67; © Alla Kazantseva / Alamy, pg. 68; Lane Oatey / Blue Jean Images / Getty Images, pg. 68; © Hero Images / Corbis, pg. 68; © Tetra Images / Alamy, pg. 68; © Image Source Plus / Alamy, pg. 68; Rhienna Cutler / Getty Images, pg. 68; DrGrounds / Getty Images, pg. 68; StockLite / Shutterstock, pg. 68; Alfonso Vicente / Alamy, pg. 68; © moodboard / Alamy, pg. 70; steven mayatt / Shutterstock, pg. 70; John Harper / Getty Images, pg. 70; © Hero Images / Corbis, pg. 70; Lane Oatey / Blue Jean Images / Getty Images, pg. 70; Fabrice LEROUGE / Getty Images, pg. 70; DrGrounds / Getty Images, pg. 70; Fuse / Getty Images, pg. 71; © Buzzshotz / Alamy, pg. 71; Nadya Lukic / Getty Images, pg. 71; Robert Deutschman / Getty Images, pg. 73; Tetra Images / Getty Images, pg. 74; © moodboard / Corbis, pg. 74; Georgijevic / iStockphoto, pg. 74; © Image Source Plus / Alamy, pg. 74; © Buero Monaco / Corbis, pg. 75; Siri Stafford / Getty Images, pg. 76; WDG Photo / Shutterstock, pg. 76; © John Lund / Marc Romanelli / Blend Images / Corbis, pg. 76; Tetra Images - Jamie Grill / Getty Images, pg. 76; © JAUBERT IMAGES / Alamy, pg. 76; © iPhone / Alamy, pg. 76; Lonely Planet / Getty Images, pg. 76; Blend Images - JGI/Jamie Grill / Getty Images, pg. 77; © Aurora Photos / Alamy, pg. 79; © Caro / Alamy, pg. 79; ingmar wesemann / Getty Images, pg. 81; Andresr / Shutterstock, pg. 95; © John Henley / Blend Images / Corbis, pg. 95; quavondo / iStockphoto, pg. 95; Rich Legg / Getty Images, pg. 96; Westend61 / Getty Images, pg. 96; Andresr / Shutterstock, pg. 98; © John Henley / Blend Images / Corbis, pg. 98; quavondo / iStockphoto, pg. 98; Rich Legg / Getty Images, pg. 99; Westend61 / Getty Images, pg. 99; © Radius Images / Alamy, pg. 101; © Radius Images / Alamy, pg. 104.